HOME RULE
VS
CORPORATE RULE

RESET FOR THE COMMON GOOD

BY

PAUL DESLAURIERS

WWW.HOMERULE.US

I

NRG PUBLISHING

P.O. Box 606

Makawoa, HI 96768

Special discounts are available on quantity purchases.
For requests, contact Info@HomeRule.US

BOOK GENRE:

Social Change

Community Organizing

Political Reform

ISBN: 978-0-9771833-4-0

DEDICATION

To Hawaiian activists who support justice and the common good.

To all activists who take a stand against the oppression of Elite Corporate Rule.

ACKNOWLEDGMENTS

The primary political action discussed in this book was aided by over 200 Maui Pono Network activists from Maui, Hawaii. A core team has been instrumental in implementing the Home Rule strategy: Bruce Douglas, Sylvia Litchfield, Daniel Smith, Ann Pitcaith and Aja Eyer. Linda Jay provided professional editing, and Bill Grieves added his cover design skills.

TABLE OF CONTENTS

CHAPTER 3 - THE TRIGGER FOR SYSTEMIC CHANGE......67

CHAPTER 4 - LISTEN TO THE PAST TO UNDERSTAND THE PRESENT......83

CHAPTER 5 - ACHIEVING HOME RULE.....113

CHAPTER 6 - THE PRIMARY BATTLE...BELIEFS...........................175

APPENDIX A   - SOCIAL ENGINEERING..209

APPENDIX B - FALSE FLAG ATTACKS............231

REFERENCES...252

INTRODUCTION

危机

The Chinese word for "crisis" consists of two syllables. The first means a dangerous moment. Our global society is in danger. Our personal liberties are in a tailspin in this Pandemic era. The second syllable means change point or crucial point when something begins or changes. Main-stream media is touting that we are in a societal reset. So, the question is what are we resetting into?

Regardless of whether you perceive this influenza virus as a terrible natural disaster, or something fabricated to enslave the population, the societal shift is in full swing. We are in a reset with lockdowns, masks, the demolition of the economy, and fear of the unknown. However, if we act quickly and strategically, we can shift to systems that benefit the common good instead of corporate profits. By acting now, we can prevent what many predict is the onset of George Orwell's *1984*,[1] and instead create a paradise on earth.

In a societal reframing, what takes hold depends on the path taken: Home Rule or Corporate Rule. Actively engaged in the reset are the corporate elite, who control the vast majority of the wealth and media. A New World Order is being declared, but what type of

"Order" are we being herded into? Technological advances of facial recognition, surveillance, 5G, and censoring the Internet. Now we have a range of medical marshal law and are being coerced to be injected with an experimental vaccine. These are just some of the tools that facilitate the few to rule the many, and a platform for the operation of a fascist police state. There is an uplifting counter-reframing that is facilitated by understanding what we are presently immersed in.

This text uncovers the formation and development of Corporate Rule in the United States. It provides a deep understanding of the characteristics of this system, and the strategies of the corporate elite. Our global society is presently wired to channel resources and control to the elite few. This is well-illustrated by wealth disparity. In 2017, an Oxfam study found that eight rich people, six of them Americans, own as much combined wealth as half the human race. In this pandemic, three people alone have raked in $84 billion dollars in personal profit, while the majority of the planet suffers.[2]

Just as the corporate elite are proactive in this reset, so must the 99% be, if we are to prevent greater restrictions on our liberty. Citizens must be willing to engage on a grassroots level in order to counter the bleak future that corporate rule brings.

But what are we engaging in? How can we assure a society that supports the common good? How can we end corrupt corporate governance? What can bring about this transition with the least amount of resistance and disruption? Can this reset for the common good be achieved in a loving and peaceful way?

The answers start by realizing we are dealing with a systems issue. It is about the wiring and control of resources and power along key paths within the system. These systems are a societal circuitry, analogous to electrical circuits that channel, amplify, dissipate, and modulate energy, and how it is used Through an understanding of this societal wiring, and the development and nature of Corporate Rule, we can go after the system's weaknesses for the most significant impact.

As an organizational development consultant for thirty-six years, my specialty was transforming organizational systems, so they perform at an optimal level. Every organized system has a key trigger point, the point within the system that can uplift and optimize it with the least amount of energy and disruption. This is also true for our much larger societal systems.

Home Rule vs Corporate Rule identifies our society's trigger and proven ways to shift it to serve the common good. Home Rule results in a system where community and environmental needs are prioritized over corporate profits and destructive policies. It is a shift from a hierarchical framework of control to the distribution of more power to a localized base. This is not about anarchy; it is about utilizing the existing system so that it serves the people, instead of supporting corporate greed and the removal of liberties. The pandemic has provided a rapid acceleration to enact Corporate Rule. This can also be an acceleration for Home Rule.

By understanding the wiring of the present system, the trigger for systemic change becomes clear. This trigger is also where grassroots have the biggest advantage, and Elite Corporate Systems have the greatest disadvantage. Our societal trigger point is located

3

within your local county, city and town. Understanding the playing field reveals a strategy to effectively and efficiently shift to the common good -- through that trigger.

The application of this strategy started in Maui County, Hawaii. Maui became a Paradise Lost in the 1800s, when the sovereign Hawaiian nation was overthrown and then blanketed by systems designed to enrich the few at the cost of the many. The same system is currently casting its dark shadow over much of this planet. It is a fascinating story, with many relevant insights on our present-day situation. Everything changed in 2018, when an effective strategy ended 125 years of corporate rule.

Because of our success, big money came back with a vengeance. In 2020, out-of-county big-money corporations spent 43 times the amount of money our local progressive group had. Although they endorsed the exact opposite of what we were supporting, we won 14 of 16 candidates and charter amendments. Grassroots and truth can easily beat big money and propaganda. We were able to do that both before and after the pandemic. It's very doable in your local area as well, even with restrictions.

The primary challenge and battle in making system change is within each of us. Propaganda, fake news and generations of conditioning are some of the tools used by the Corporate Elite to lull society into a trance with fabricated and distorted stories that place a veil over facts and intentions. This book lifts off that veil and empowers you to create a bright future.

The Appendix explores important topics, such as the many facets of social engineering and propaganda and ways to diminish their effect. Also, "False Flag Attacks" that are used to create a crisis and then provide solutions that further reduce liberties and extract tremendous wealth from the masses, is a well-worn tactic we all should be aware of, especially with what our global society is facing.

These engaging insights could lead to a local community venture that can positively impact you, your family and future generations. Gaining local control for the common good is doable and is being achieved currently in pockets. We can create societal systems that serve the people instead of corporate profits. This democracy is not a far-fetched vision, but rather a clear goal that is achievable by using both the facts and this empowering guide to systemic change.

The most effective approach to rid our nation of this exploitive, manipulative, unjust hierarchy is at the grassroots level, where we still have power. By becoming informed, we can direct this grassroots energy to the trigger that can rapidly, effectively, and with little disruption change our societal system to serve the common good.

CHAPTER 1

THE ELITE CORPORATE SYSTEM

Shifting from Elite Corporate Rule to Home Rule is a systems issue. By understanding the system that shapes society, we can effectively transform it. As an organizational development and systems engineer, I would map the processes, structure and interpersonal dynamics of an organization as a wiring diagram exhibiting its energy flow.

This facilitated an objective holistic view of the organized system. From this perspective, the major accessible point generating dysfunction and blocks affecting performance became obvious. This point I refer to as a "trigger" that can rapidly transform the system. There is always a trigger point within any organized system. Shifting that one point triggers the entire system to function at a much higher level of effectiveness and fulfillment. In business, the trigger can be a leader who does not listen, short-circuited resource distribution, an executive team at odds with each other, a culture of back-stabbing and gossip, territorial struggles between department heads, or a missing

7

component in their development. A trigger is described in detail in one of my previous publications: *IN THE HIGH-ENERGY ZONE: The 6 Characteristics of Highly Effective Groups.*[3]

A system sustained and developed for over a hundred years has structures, values and mechanisms that sustain and develop it. Control over society is maintained within this structured system. There are certain characteristics of this system that expose its operation and show its weakness, providing an informed strategy.

This chapter provides a depiction of the structure and interpersonal dynamics of Corporate Rule. We must understand it if we are to transform it. Taking an objective look at recent history and sticking with facts is very revealing. Let us explore the development of Corporate Rule, its characteristics and the primary strategies used to fulfill its agenda.

Explore the past to understand what has emerged in the present.

INCEPTION AND DEVELOPMENT OF CORPORATE RULE

Corporate Elites in the United States have been attempting to enslave and exploit the working class and their labor since the white man settled in. In 1910, the foundation was laid that would transform our societal system and greatly accelerated the Elite's control.

The nation's most powerful bankers met secretly off the coast of Georgia, on Jekyll Island, drafting a proposal for a private Central Banking system that would become the Federal Reserve.

The bankers supported Woodrow Wilson's presidential candidacy. Once in office, he actually successfully staged an overthrow of this nation's monetary system; the ramifications of this ploy later showed its cancerous infection.

In December 1913, while many members of Congress were home for Christmas, the Federal Reserve Act was rammed through Congress and signed by President Wilson.

The Fed became law the day before Christmas Eve in 1913. It was one of those backdoor deals, making sure those who opposed it were not present. Shortly afterwards, the German International bankers Kuhn, Loeb and Co. sent one of their partners there to run the Fed.

The Federal Reserve Act allowed the Central Bankers to win a long-fought battle. Now they were able to create money and loan it out at interest, make decisions without government approval, and control the amount of money in circulation, creating bubbles of inflation and busts of depressions at their will.

The Initial Primary Owners of the Federal Reserve Bank

1. Rothschild's of London and Berlin
2. Lazard Brothers of Paris
3. Israel Moses Seaf of Italy
4. Kuhn, Loeb & Co. of Germany and New York
5. Warburg & Company of Hamburg, Germany
6. Lehman Brothers of New York
7. Goldman, Sachs of New York
8. Rockefeller Brothers of New York

Also, in 1913 the U.S. government changed the taxation system so that instead of corporate profits, the tax base shifted to personal income. Since the Constitution only allowed direct apportioned taxation amongst the States, indirect Income Tax was initiated through the 16th Amendment, which was pushed through, in February 1913.

World War I conveniently happened in 1914. The Federal Reserve profited handsomely. That is when U.S. banks became a creditor nation instead of a debtor nation. By 1917, American loans to the Allies had soared to $2.25 billion; loans to Germany stood at a paltry $27 million. The USA's prominence to power as the provider of the significant world currency was established. Bankers profited greatly from borrowing and reconstruction in the wake of the war.

In 1929, the Federal Reserve began to pull money out of circulation as loans were paid back. Between 1929 and 1933, the Federal Reserve reduced the money supply by 33%. [4] With significantly less money to go around, businessmen could not get new loans and could not even get their old loans renewed, forcing many to stop investing. The Federal Reserve, especially the New York branch,[5] created a "bust" -- which was inevitable after issuing so much credit in the years before. The Federal Reserve's actions triggered the banking crisis, which led to the Great Depression.

Who profited from the Great Depression?...The Banksters. This depression, initiated by the Federal Reserve Bank, transferred billions of dollars into the private bankers" hands at the expense and the impoverishment of nearly everyone else.

11

Wealth translates to power, which brings more wealth and even more power. From this foothold, it began to spread to a variety of institutions, oil, pharmaceuticals, education, like a cancer out of control, infecting more and more of the systems and morphing into a horrible sickness of wealth disparity and the subtle manipulation and domination of citizens.

Power and money provide the means to change legislation, such as tax distribution, deregulation, and corporate governance. These means are used to elect officials like Woodrow Wilson. The architects of society rig it for themselves.

World War II generated an even stronger needs for finances, as devastated nations sought help to rebuild from the ravages of war. The US oil-backed dollar became the monetary ruler of the planet.

Based on the successes in intelligence-gathering in World War II, this growing shadow government felt justified in pushing their legislatures to form the National Security Council. Under the provisions of the National Security Act of 1947, the National Security Council (NSC) and the Central Intelligence Agency (CIA) were created. The Act charged the CIA with coordinating the nation's intelligence activities and correlating, evaluating, and disseminating intelligence that affects national security. The CIA was also authorized to conduct clandestine operations.

12

This then gave an important mechanism to Corporate Rule; they could use tax payer money to support their growing foreign policy. Their connections with the MOSSAD in Israel, and MI-6 in Great Britain, who enhanced their eyes and ears, and a channel to carry out covert operations ... operations that always are in the interest of the Elite few. Their empire is largely built on the manipulation of information and on covert operations.

1953 - IRAN AND THE CIA

The CIA's first coup d'état was the overthrow of the democratically elected government of Iran. Prime Minister Mohammad Mosaddegh began nationalizing the country's oil reserves in 1953, when he followed through on his election promises. The oil industry of Iran was then controlled by the Anglo-Iranian Oil Company, whose refinery is shown in this photo.

The CIA was sent into Iran to bring an end to Mosaddegh 's government.[6] The coup was orchestrated by the intelligence agencies of the United Kingdom and the United States.

The CIA bribed street thugs, clergy, politicians and Iranian army officers to take part in a propaganda campaign against Mosaddegh and his government. According to the CIA's declassified documents and records, some of the most feared mobsters in Tehran were hired by the CIA to stage pro-Shah riots on August 19. Other CIA-paid provocateurs were brought into Tehran in buses and trucks and took over the streets of the city. They began a campaign of terror, staging bombings and attacks on Muslim targets in order to blame them on Mosaddegh. They fostered and funded an anti-Mosaddegh campaign amongst the radical Islamist elements in the country. 800 people were killed during, and as a direct result of, the conflict. Finally, they backed the revolution that brought their favorite puppet, the Shah, into power.[7]

Within months, their mission had been accomplished: they had removed a democratically elected leader who threatened to build up an independent, secular Persian nation and had replaced him with a repressive tyrant whose secret police would brutally suppress all opposition.

Mosaddegh was arrested, tried and convicted of treason by the Shah's military court. He was sentenced to three years in jail, and then placed under house arrest for the remainder of his life. Mosaddegh's supporters were rounded up and either imprisoned, tortured or executed. Among the tangible benefits the Elite reaped from overthrowing Iran's elected government was a share of Iran's oil wealth. Washington continued to supply arms to the unpopular Shah, and the CIA-trained SAVAK, his repressive secret police force. The Shah ruled as an authoritarian monarch for the next 26 years, until he was overthrown in a popular revolt by the residents in 1979.

According to the CIA, the campaign was a success; the after-action report described the operation in glowing terms. The pattern was repeated time and time again in country after country: Guatemala, Laos, the Dominican Republic, Ecuador, Brazil, Indonesia, Greece, Bolivia ... and the list goes on to the more recent Afghanistan, Iraq, and Libya invasions.

EISENHOWER'S WARNING TO THE AMERICAN PEOPLE

The citizens of the U.S. were warned by Dwight Eisenhower during his presidential farewell speech to the nation on January 17, 1961. *"We face a hostile ideology--global in scope, atheistic in character, ruthless in purpose, and insidious in method. Unhappily, the danger it poses promises to be of indefinite duration....*

This conjunction of an immense military establishment and a large arms industry is new in the American experience. The total influence-economic, political, even spiritual--is felt in every city, every statehouse, every office of the federal government. We recognize the imperative need for this development. Yet we must not fail to comprehend its grave implications. Our toil, resources and livelihood are all involved; so is the very structure of our society.

In the councils of government, we must guard against the acquisition of unwarranted influence, whether sought or unsought, by the military-industrial complex. The potential for the disastrous rise of misplaced power exists and will persist.

We must never let the weight of this combination endanger our liberties or democratic processes. We should take nothing for granted. Only an alert and knowledgeable citizenry can compel the proper meshing of the huge industrial and military machinery of defense with our peaceful methods and goals, so that security and liberty may prosper together."

But over the years, the power has been misplaced; the only security being sought is to secure greater wealth for the ultra-wealthy. The citizenry has not been alert or knowledgeable. Under this regime, they have been dismantling liberty on a global scale. Notice how it doesn't matter if a Democrat or Republican is in power; the same policy of global subjugation continues.

In the post-war economy, the United States thrived because in part, its lands and population were not laid waste by the war's devastation. This was also fueled by the GI Bill and benefits of the New Deal. By the 1950s and 1960s, the United States' middle class blossomed, with free education, good manufacturing jobs, and a wide variety of professions that paid well. This was still a racist system, which made it more difficult for minorities to be in that middle class. For many, one breadwinner could afford to support a family of five, providing a good education for his or her children and a comfortable house, with retirement savings. The American Dream was real, as it was for my family.

Then people began to wake up to the corrupt system and the military industrial complex's lust for war. During that time, the number of protests and demands for change was growing, and the Elite felt they were losing control to democracy. Women's rights, civil rights protests, college demonstrations against the Vietnam War, unions gaining workers' rights, and new forms of social systems made it appear the Elites' control was slipping through their fingers. When they faced opposition to their dominance, the Elites increased control and regulations while lowering wages and greatly increasing their own profits.

The backlash, which has been devastating, illustrates how the Corporate Elite System pulls its levers to manipulate our societal systems in a relatively short time in order to change the fortunes of the vast majority. They changed the systems to reduce both democracy and the challenge to their control and dominance. Sound familiar with what we are presently facing?

The 1% attacked the wages. Between 1969 and 2009, the median wages earned by American men between the ages of 30 and 50 dropped by 27% after inflation. Between 1973 and 2007, the average U.S. non-supervisory wage, adjusted for inflation, dropped by 18 percent. [8] This was during a time when automation has greatly increased worker productivity. An average worker needs to work a mere 11 hours a week to produce as much as a worker putting in 40 hours per week in 1950. [92] Being four times as productive results in a pay cut for the workers, while the leaders increase their salary nearly 100 times and provide a windfall for investors and bankers.

The Elite changed the playing field, so laborers now compete with world markets. This provided the leverage to destroy unions, making the population fearful about job insecurity. Outsourcing American jobs to foreign countries in the name of corporate profit has left blue-collar workers struggling just to feed their families. Back in 1980, less than 30% of all jobs in the United States were low-income jobs. In 2019, the number of people earning less than $30,000 accounts for 46.5% of the population.

To add insult to injury, the Elite justify charging exorbitant interest on pieces of paper and digital entries that are fiat, nothing of value backing them. Since 1971, consumer debt in the United States has increased by a whopping 1,700 percent.[10] Inflate the cost of education, and then enslave students to a life of debt. According to the Student Loan Debt Clock, total student loan debt in the United States surpassed the 1 trillion-dollar mark in 2012. Americans owed over $1.56 trillion in student loan debt in 2019. That is again part of the stress to prevent the college uprising that occurred in the 1970s. Now in this present "reset" this trend of wealth disparity is escalating.

Only FOUR out of 150 countries have more wealth inequality than the U.S. In a world listing compiled by a reputable research team,[11] it was shown the U.S. has greater wealth inequality than every measured country in the world except for Namibia, Zimbabwe, Denmark, and Switzerland. It is even more alarming to consider global statistics. Imagine: .01% of the population control 81% of the world's wealth.

Let's look at this system in action. U.S. billionaires saw their fortunes soar by $434 billion during the nation's lockdown between mid-March and mid-May 2020, according to a new report: *Forbes* data for America's more than 600 billionaires between March 18, when most states were in lockdown, and May 19. Bezos, who owns Amazon, leads the league. His net worth grew by $25 billion from January 1 through mid-April, 2020—while 20 million U.S. workers lost their jobs in those same weeks. The collective wealth of all U.S. billionaires has increased over $1.1 trillion since mid-March 2020, a nearly 40% leap during the past 10 months of national emergency.

Now we have Bill Gates of Microsoft fame telling us that the entire planet needs to take an injection that is not a vaccine that uses antigens to trigger an immune repose, but actually is a biological agent. Oh, and by the way there have been no conclusive clinical trials, it is experimental. One of the primary manufacturers Glaxo Smith Kline has a history of doing harm and paid $7.9 Billion in fines for injuring people. And one more thing, the pharmaceutical industry cannot be held liable, the tax-payers are.

How can we escape the reset planned under Corporate Rule? The shift begins with understanding what we are dealing with. This type of corporate rule and fascism is pervasive within the vast majority systems that run global society. This is not hyperbole. The corporate system's lifeblood is a fiat currency that they control. It relies on manipulation and deception. For this system to develop and evolve since 1913 there must be something binding a certain structure and framework for this operation to be sustained. That binding structure has certain characteristics.

In 2010, the U.S. Supreme Court, in Citizens United v. Federal Election Commission, ruled that the government cannot restrict independent expenditures by corporations or unions to political campaigns. This further strengthened the growing grip of corporate personhood.

Corporate lawyers (acting as both attorneys and judges) subverted our Bill of Rights in the late 1800s by establishing the doctrine of "corporate personhood" — the claim that corporations were intended to fully enjoy the legal status and protections created for human beings. So, a description of this person's character is telling.

HIERARCHY

This is a structure that consolidates power and wealth at the top. A pyramid shape facilitates control by a few. The pyramid structure indicates how control of the masses is vested in a few. In ancient Egypt, the top of the societal structure was never questioned, as the Pharaohs were considered gods. The division of ministers and priests allowed the leaders' orchestration of the nation's people and resources. The Pharaohs' reign was in harmony with the people, nature, and a higher power. Their pyramid was connected in a continuous whole. The Pharaohs were responsive to all their connections. Perhaps that is why they reigned for 2,800 years.

In our present ruling system, the pyramid is disconnected at the top. There is a separation from the needs of the environment and citizens, and a focus on their own self- contained agenda. The goals of those who control this top pyramid are not the betterment of the human race, or for the masses to reach their potential. They are about creating and reinforcing a system that furthers their own agenda of control and domination. The signature of these systems is that they consolidate power at the top and are secretive. The entire system structure of the Elite is based on a wiring that allows control by a few, while they are unanswerable to the 99%.

Also, within the circuitry of this system are what I call amplifiers, which one finds in any hierarchical structure. Hierarchical organizations reflect and amplify the values, convictions and intentions of those who have and utilize the main power authority and influence. For example, if systemic racism exists and there is a disenfranchisement of blacks and Latinos, then it reflects the top. It is a separatist consciousness where the elite few see others as below them and inferior. It is a eugenicist's perspective that elevates the rich and powerful as God's heirs to control and rule the lowly 99%. This is a separatist's consciousness that sees the masses as prey and "sheeple." The suffering they wrought is of no concern, it's just collateral damage. The symbol of the separated pyramid on the one-dollar bill says it all.

CONSOLIDATION AND BACK-DOOR DEALS

The nature of this overreaching hierarchical framework is to consolidate and control from the top down. The Elite are always trying to get their competitors; battles on the upper levels of the pyramid often occur as they play the Monopoly game. That means infighting and destructive battles are fought among the Elite, which often leaves enemies in their wake. Eventually, they monopolize for their profit and control.

Back-door deals are part of the scam. Agreements, plans and strategies are made behind closed doors, benefiting the people and their associates behind those doors. They limit inclusion and rig things for their own benefit. Those excluded have something to rally around, developing opposition. Exclusion from the deals can lead to infighting.

With corporate lobbyists lurking in the halls of Congress and the Senate who help craft deals, campaign contributions are made. Lobbyists for the corporations write legislation that benefits their employer and is then taken up by the politicians, who often share the same benefactor. The passed laws further benefit and strengthen the growing fascism. This is all laid out as "business as usual," but there is nothing normal about a system that allows the foxes to run the henhouse!

A clear example is mainstream media. Control of the media is essential to engineer consent. When I was a business consultant, I worked closely with 28 TV broadcasting stations from 1987 to 1993. I dined with broadcasting executives who often expressed their

23

concerns about the Federal Communication Commission (FCC) regulation changes. There were an alarming number of mergers and buyouts, and they were seeing the repercussions in their industry. The only groups to win these merger bids were large corporate entities run by right-wing extremists. These executives knew that when diversity is lost, and the group controlling the media has an extremist agenda, our ability to get to the truth will be greatly diminished.

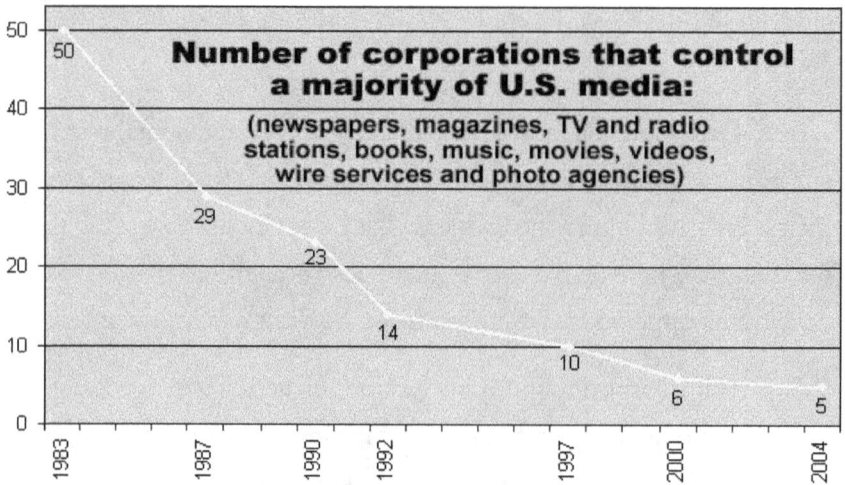

Number of corporations that control a majority of U.S. media:

(newspapers, magazines, TV and radio stations, books, music, movies, videos, wire services and photo agencies)

Year	Number
1983	50
1987	29
1990	23
1992	14
1997	10
2000	6
2004	5

In 1983, 50 corporations controlled the vast majority of all news media in the U.S. At the time, Ben Bagdikian was called "alarmist" for pointing this out in his book, *The Media Monopoly.* These corporations owned and operated 90% of the mass media— controlling almost all of America's newspapers, magazines, TV and radio stations, books, records, movies, videos, wire services and photo agencies. In 2004, Bagdikian's revised and expanded book, *The New Media Monopoly,* shows that only five huge corporations — Time Warner, Disney, Murdoch's News Corporation, Bertelsmann of

Germany, and Viacom (formerly CBS) — now control most of the media industry in the U.S. General Electric's NBC is a close sixth.

It is not only that the top-down control of the news makes up or distorts stories; it is that journalists are being complicit. As the vehicle through which information from the outside world is captured, sorted, edited and transmitted into our homes, the mass media has a huge responsibility. It shapes and informs our understanding of events to which we don't have first-hand access. A large portion of the investigative journalists are no longer in the industry. Now we get talking heads with scripts handed down from above.

This is especially disturbing when you realize the pandemic fear being generated and the constant drumbeat to take the "vaccine" shot. The Internet is being censored, removing many factual reports that oppose the mainstream narrative. Information on vaccines risks and the content of these shots, actual death rates from the pandemic, facts about testing methods, are removed. Studies on the effectiveness of wearing masks and lock-downs, and solid, scientific, well-researched findings are scrubbed. Why is important information being blocked on Main Street media, social media and Internet? Why are we being fed a narrative that does not coincide with facts? Realize the present consolidation of the media outlets allows control of the narrative as opposing stories are eliminated with repetition of what the Corporate Rulers want people to believe.

Aside for a few pockets of truthful reporters, like CorbettReport.com, a major portion of Main Street media is shaped by the Corporate Elite and their agenda. As a result, fake news and propaganda provides a distorted sense of reality. Look at the Trump

25

vs. Democratic Party Russian probe, even if it was contrived, it engaged a nation. Reflect on the amount of news coverage this received, only to amount to nothing except distraction.

COMPARTMENTALIZE, AND SECRECY

The structure divides tasks among their minions, assuring that the Elite few understand the big picture. It takes a lot of energy to be deceptive and hide the truth. However, when you develop hierarchy, you add layers to the pyramid, which can easily translate into a long bureaucratic maze with blocks along the way.

A long path of requirements, approvals, and provisions make any substantive change from the bottom of the pyramid impossible. Layers of compartmentalization complicate the true picture of what is occurring. Operations are divided into tasks and functions, so few can see the big picture. Layers of bureaucracy often hide the true perpetrators, and, most importantly, fracture the pieces of the plan, so only a few get a true picture of what is going on. Each department controlling a single piece leaves only the executive team to see how it all works together. This reduces the number of those who know the true strategy, decreasing the probability of a leak, and also makes its source difficult to trace.

There are disadvantages to this wiring. Layers of empowerment and approval can make reaction-and-response slow.

Commands and details can be short-circuited anywhere along the chain of command. There is a built-in mechanism that slows reaction-and-response time.

When dissent about the imbalance in the system is expressed in peaceful ways, media distorts the numbers of participants at protests; saboteurs are brought in to incite violence among the peaceful protestors and justify crackdowns. It is a repeated theme globally. The role of protests can promote a progressive narrative. However, the system is blocked as you go up the pyramid.

Elite Systems provide the illusion of citizen participation and choice. In reality, money controllers have power over deciding who will be the next political star to carry out their will. Citizens have less power than they think, because of the way the election system is wired. Yet there are some representatives for the people that do get in office.

In the Corporate Elite System, secrecy and closed-door operations are often how decisions are made and policy develops. Dennis Kucinich, a former U.S. Representative from Ohio who served from 1997 to 2013, was a champion of the people. I interviewed him on a radio show, and he described that while he was on the finance committee, how they would exclude him from their back-door deal making sessions. His aides would sniff out the meeting, and then he would casually walk in the room immediately, changing the entire tenor of the meeting. He simply declared that there must have been a problem with the notification, apologized for being late, and sat down as those present awkwardly stumbled on.

A smokescreen of supposedly complicated negotiations, bi-partisan fighting, and deals becomes the excuse for the policies. Or a crisis is created so the Corporate Elite can implement their plan as part of a deceptive solution. Our present crisis has solutions being proposed that would have horrific consequences to our liberties.

The ultra-elite are well-hidden from public view. They hire front people to create the illusion that their puppets are in control. Through massive holdings, the Elite compartmentalize components of businesses, creating layers to hide the real power brokers. They also hire front people to create the illusion that their puppets are in control. A good example is J.P. Morgan, considered one of the wealthiest Americans of the 1920s. When his will was publicly revealed, it was shown that he was a mere front person for the Rothschild Empire.

The Elite creates organizations they invest with power and keep control of. Some examples are the Federal Reserve, Tri-Lateral Commission, Council on Foreign Relations, and the International Monetary Fund. Significant efforts go into creating overarching mechanisms that consolidate military power, governance and currency.

Steps of individual advancement translate into steps of ever-increasing allegiance to these organizations. If that loyalty is not kept, the consequences are significant and discourage any disclosure. CIA agents who confided in me made it clear that if the source was traced, both they and I would be dead.

The declared war on terror made any significant information on black ops or the deep state shielded under "national security," making the veil of secrecy thick and opaque. Truth-tellers are persecuted. Julian Paul Assange is an Australian editor, publisher, and activist who founded WikiLeaks in 2006. WikiLeaks came to international attention in 2010 when it published a series of leaks provided by U.S. Army intelligence analyst Chelsea Manning. Assange, 49, has been in custody or self-imposed exile in London for the better part of a decade. He initially sought refuge in the Ecuadorian embassy in 2012. The U.S. government is still after him.

A growing number of people see that the U.S. government and the corporate world have secretly fused together in a scheme to misinform the public and relegate the population to serfdom. Their collaboration provides a power that no individual can go up against. However, when a portion of the 99% come together, they generate a force that can eliminate this exploitation, and install systems that benefit the community and the common good.

LOYALTY ABOVE ETHICS AND DARK VALUES

In a hierarchy, those who have and utilize the main powers, authority and influence, shape the organization and the systems that constitute its functioning. If those in power use deception, secrecy, propaganda, theft, divisiveness, and harm others, the resulting systems will reflect that behavior.

The most important qualification of membership and rising in this system is loyalty. Participation is first built on loyalty, not competence. Members must carry out orders and must go through an arduous process of proving their allegiance through different levels as they advance in this Elite System. Look into their ties with big money and how they make decisions for their overlords; that makes those individuals, including politicians, easy to identify.

The rise to the upper levels requires embracing Dark Values that include deception, manipulation, lies, greed, theft, self-centered delusion, and even murder. Those who rise to the top have their moral compass pointed toward their profit and power. It has the character of a mafia-type organization where secrecy is part of the deeds against humanity. They employ evil and domination as core values.

Some decide to break away from Dark Values, and there are repercussions. Look at what happens to whistle-blowers like Eric Snowden. He alerted U.S. citizens about the National Security Agency (NSA) surveillance program, that all of your pictures, emails, phone calls are being recorded and stored. It has now been ruled unlawful, seven years after it was exposed by Snowden. After being denied asylum by 27 nations in 2013, he settled in Russia, where he remains today. Even though he informed the public of the extensive spying on them, it has been ruled unlawful, yet the practice is still in full swing. With 5G that surveillance is intensified.

This system is based on divisiveness and opposing others, secrecy, theft, lies and manipulation. It is how mafias function. But this is a much more powerful system fueled by Corporate Rule.

SOCIOPATHIC SYSTEM

The personalities that thrive in these systems are sociopaths, who make up about 4% of the general population. Under this category are psychopaths, who are more socially unstable and make up about 1% of the general population. In this Corporate Elite System, sociopaths rise quickly through the ranks, in part based on how they align with dark values. People who embrace the system soon exhibit the behavior.

Sociopaths have "emotional deafness" — a biochemical inability to experience normal feelings of empathy for others. There is an insular focus on personal desires. This shark-like fixation on self-interest means that sociopaths often feel a clear detachment from other people, viewing them more as small animals to be preyed upon than as fellow humans to relate to.

They lack compassion and only think of themselves — *"all for me and none for you."* They see themselves as above others; the rules do not apply to them. *"I can do what I please."* According to them, they are the rulers of these lowly serfs. They see themselves as superior. However, the truth is very different. They have not evolved to a collaborative and mutually supportive consciousness.

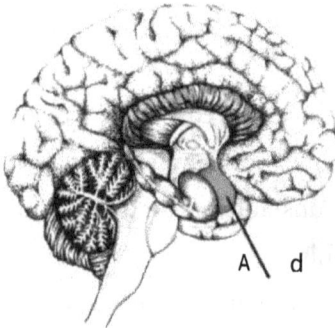

It is as if the reptilian part of their brain, the Amygdala, dominates, like lizards, who lack compassion and eat their young. Some sociopaths and many psychopaths actually have a genetically inherited biochemical condition that prevents them from feeling normal human empathy.

We must realize the mindset of the oppressor. This consciousness is capable of atrocities much greater than most people realize is possible. Most people can't imagine that this "democratic" system can house evil. 96% of the population's consciousness is not wired to do such harm for profit. The unimaginable is one of their biggest veils.

Many are eugenicists, who see themselves above the masses needing to rule lower forms of life. They see common folk as cannon fodder. It is a separatist consciousness devoid of compassion that gives them permission to do as they please without remorse.

The Elite's most profitable venture is war. They get to charge the taxpayer exorbitant prices for the weapons they manufacture and explode. They get to cause great harm to a country and their people, steal their resources, charge exorbitant prices for fixing the infrastructure they just destroyed, and then the IMF (International Monetary Fund) charges interest to further enslave the remaining population in debt. Finally, residents get to live in fear as drones fly overhead with their deadly payloads.

So, we are presently dealing with sociopathic systems. Just as this personality type consistently exhibits particular fears and concerns, the systems made in their image share the same vulnerabilities. The two biggest fears of a sociopath and the more severe psychopaths are (1) being found out and (2) losing power. This makes two strategies stand out: inform the public of the deception, and unplug from these evil systems. It is doable when you understand the system, its power base and how to change it from the inside out.

Here are a few key aspects of sociopathic systems. First, they are based on divisiveness and opposing others, theft, secrecy, lies and manipulation. It is the glue that binds together this house of cards. If people were aware of their diabolical systems and deceptions, they would vote them all out of office, and the house of cards would collapse. So, exposure of the truth is their biggest enemy and fear. That is why they have gone to such great lengths to control the mainstream media and the Internet.

SOCIAL ENGINEERING

There are a wide variety of weapons used by the elite to subjugate society. Realize we are referring to a group that does not have the same moral compass. In their world anything goes, there are no rules, just winning. Their weapons include monetary manipulation and divisiveness, that were already mentioned; however, their two most sinister weapons are social engineering and false flag attacks. They are mentioned here, and are further illustrated in Appendices A and B.

What is the major weapon that allows the control of global society by an elite few? How are the citizens deluded into thinking that what is occurring is normal? What prevents the 99% from uprising and changing the systems to reclaim their sovereign rights?

Any social order based on inequality of wealth or power depends on repression and deception to control the disadvantaged majority. A key weapon that takes many forms is in our media and our education system. There has been a social construct going on for generations. It is a science skillfully developed to shape your beliefs, the main battle for systemic change.

Underneath all we perceive is all we believe. Our subconscious beliefs serve as an ever-active filter for what we see, and the actions we take. It affects all we perceive from our environment, shaping our thoughts and actions.

Our unconscious beliefs and collective unconscious provide a framework for our life, and what we see as real. Inculcated for generations, our reality has been shaped since birth. The collective unconscious generates and reinforces perceptions and culture.

Étienne de La Boétie described the dilemma some 500 years ago and it holds true today: *The Politics of Obedience: The Discourse of Voluntary Servitude*, the 16th- century treatise on tyranny and obedience.[12] A conclusion is that it is cultural conditioning and the known that keep people following despotic rulers -- despite their ability to overthrow the exploitive system.

Beliefs and the community narrative are malleable and can be revised by repeated images and messages. In many ways, we are programmed to see the world in a certain way. Repeated themes include: The United States stands for democracy and freedom, do as you're told during the pandemic, the terrorists are out to get us, pay your mortgage and taxes, strive for the American Dream ... blah, blah, blah! If we are brought up in an environment where our parents, siblings, and friends all believe the same thing, it becomes part of our collective beliefs and perceptions.

Beliefs can be planted in our subconscious without our knowledge or consent. These distorted beliefs act as filters that narrow and delude our perception. They can be shaped by social engineering, involving a wide range of media, particularly television. We can be led to believe anything, including the false perception that we are powerless to change these corrupt systems. Consciousness sustains the delusion; however, consciousness can also end the delusion.

Beliefs can help humanity reach its highest potential or cause its own enslavement. The primary weapons of the Elite System are the false beliefs that deceive us and prevent us from seeing a deeper truth and taking action. The analogy of battle is appropriate, as these opposing forces are invading the subconscious to deceive us into handing our wealth and well-being to a few self-proclaimed leaders. This invasion allows a sinister agenda to unfold. From the manipulation of the subconscious, we have become partially enslaved in the Elite's dream world, although most of us don't know it. The Elite's dream world reinforces fear, debt, separation, and violence.

There is a constant drumming of beliefs to reinforce the system through propaganda and deception that is broadcast through a wide variety of media platforms. The resulting subconscious implant shapes what we perceive as real. Behind that false perception is a planet ripe for the taking, for the orchestrators of these false perceptions.

Marginalize the population by having them chase trinkets and possessions. Have them fight amongst themselves for moral and racial issues. Emphasize fashion, political and celebrity dramas and the latest gadgets — instead of awareness of what is truly going on.

These beliefs become reinforced to create what is familiar. The roots of these beliefs can go deep. Individuals and societies often choose to suffer instead of letting go of the "known," or the familiar. Even if the familiar is feudalism, or wage slavery, many would prefer that than having to learn a new way of operating.

The Nazis themselves were masterful at influencing political attitudes. The Nazi propaganda machine under Joseph Goebbels was a synchronized, sophisticated and effective tool for creating public opinion. He said, *"If you tell a lie big enough and keep repeating it, people will eventually come to believe it. The lie can be maintained only for such time as the State can shield the people from the political, economic and/or military consequences of the lie. It thus becomes vitally important for the State to use all of its powers to repress dissent, for the truth is the mortal enemy of the lie, and thus by extension, the truth is the greatest enemy of the State."*

Non-authoritarian regimes, in particular, the United States, Great Britain, and Australia, tend to rely on more subtle social engineering campaigns that create more gradual, but ultimately far-reaching, change. For Corporate Rule, it is not the truth that counts, but perception. The "War on Terror" has shaped much of our foreign policy and drained the United States' coffers. Post-9/11/2001, the war on terror has cost $6.4 trillion. The manipulation of the media plays a large role in this deceit of creating an Elite/Banking/Corporate-run "false democracy" in which power brokers can flourish.

FALSE FLAG ATTACKS

Create violence, blame it on others, and then use that fear to gain more power. It has a term "Hegelian dialectic" that has three parts. 1) Give rise to a problem and blame it on others. 2) Come in with strong-arm solutions. 3) Enrich the few and further restrict the liberties of the many. This is why there are hundreds of documented examples of governments staging attacks in order to blame them on their political enemies.[13] In every civilization, in every culture, in every historical period, authoritarians have known that spectacular acts of violence help to further consolidate their own power and control.

The extent to which the Elite Corporate System will go to consolidate their profit and power is hard for most decent people to grasp. Nothing invigorates and empowers an authoritarian regime more than a spectacular act of violence and crisis.

We must look to the recent past to see the pattern of this strategy being applied today. The Elite Systems use violence and fear as their leverage for extracting freedom and wealth. The "War on Terror" has been a windfall for the Elite Few. From September 2001, that "War" has cost the US taxpayers $6.4 trillion just for expenditures related to the terror scare. Present military spending is $669 billion a year. This is just part of the motivation involved in a so-called "War on Terror."

Now we have another form of Liberty erosion and wealth distribution. There is an even greater concern now, as our entire global society is in tailspin. Follow the facts from the past to picture what is in store with the "big reset" they keep referring to.

Acts of terror and violence never benefit the average man or woman, only those in positions of power. This fact has been used for centuries. Nero fiddled while Rome burned from fires he had set, according to historians. [14] He had his scapegoats, Christians, to blame, torture, and throw to the lions. Seventy percent of the capital of the Roman Empire was rebuilt in Nero's own image, and further restrictions were made on the freedom of the citizens.

A major avenue for this aggressive approach to overtake democratically elected governments is through the International Monetary Fund, the U.S. CIA, the U.S. State Department, and multinational corporations, under the guise of democracy and freedom. Some of the greatest destruction of human life and property this world has ever seen has been perpetrated by the banker-pharmaceutical-oil barons' covert strong-arms. The CIA has sponsored terrorism in 30 countries since its inception. However, there are false flag attacks that have a profound impact on our U.S. society, and the world, today.

An example is August 1964. The public was told that the North Vietnamese had attacked a U.S. destroyer in the Gulf of Tonkin on two separate occasions. The attacks were portrayed as a clear example of "Communist aggression," and a resolution was soon passed in Congress authorizing President Johnson to begin deploying U.S. forces in Vietnam. The second attack was the primary reason cited to justify full involvement in the conflict.

However, in 2005, an internal NSA study was released, concluding that the second "attack" that provoked the war in fact never took place.[15] The war hawks simply told a lie to plunge us into a war that profited them greatly.

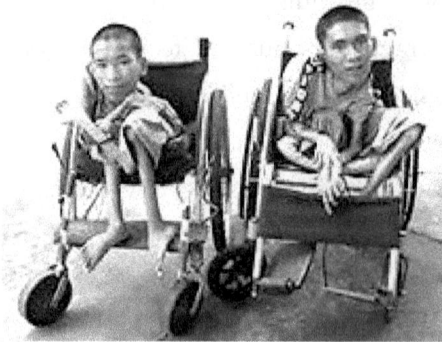

In effect, 60,000 American servicemen and as many as three million Vietnamese, and 500,000 Cambodians and Laotians, lost their lives. [16] Now consider the tens of thousands of birth defects that occurred because of Agent Orange, the toxins left on the land, and within the people who fought these wars. Let alone the mental toll on veterans and survivors. All based on a lie.

The facts and the content of the 9/11 Commission Report, the U.S. government's "official story," shows the cornerstone of the government's evidence of two planes bringing down three enormous skyscrapers (including Building 7), at free-fall speed. The collapse of the 47-story World Trade Center Building 7, a steel-framed high-rise, is highly suspicious, as no plane hit this building and was the third in history to "collapse from fires alone," the first and second being the WTC Twin Towers. How can a few small fires collapse this building at free-fall speed and have the entire building in a pile at its footprint?

An investigation is needed. Evidence pointing to the towers' collapse and the facts of the attack on the Pentagon does not match the 9/11 Commission Report. The Commission failed — there were over 100 other unanswered questions, omissions, inconsistencies and implausible scenarios. Refer to Appendix B. All efforts to get a recognized independent investigation so far have been blocked by federal courts. The "War on Terror" then was transferred to Iraq's false accusations of "Weapons of Mass Destruction" for that invasion.

We now know that in fact the stockpiles did not exist and that there were no weapons of mass destruction--except the U.S. military and their coalition, which had generated mass destruction on this sovereign country. Although the Bush administration had premeditatedly lied the country into yet another war, and yet the most intense opposition the administration ever received over this documented war crime was some polite correction on the Sunday political talk show circuit. Look at the cost in lives and wealth for those nations! Trillions of dollars have been spent and trillions of dollars are unaccounted for. The suffering caused to millions of people was unimaginable, and was all based on a lie.

False flag attacks were used in Libya. In 2011, President Obama admitted the presence of covert operatives on the ground in Libya (identified as CIA agents by the *New York Times),* as well as the goal of destabilizing the Gaddafi government. After foreign mercenaries were brought in to kill civilians, the media blamed the Libyan government for killing its own citizens. They were able to use propaganda to justify an invasion by UN allies "for humanitarian reasons." Now, the entire country has been ransacked, and disease and poverty have greatly escalated. Since the U.S. invasion, the economy and public services are decimated, including the public health system, law enforcement, and the judiciary. This has caused the internal displacement of over 200,000 people — but those truths do not make the media news.

U.S. citizens can't even question these facts. Despotism now bears the mantle of "security." People are realizing that the questioning needs to go to the highest level. This delusional veil, shrouded as security, needs to be lifted. Now, more than ever, we must wake up to the past and present.

The new weapon of medical martial law, social distancing, vaccinations and business shut-downs must be looked at with suspicion. Restricted laws and medical martial law have been active since 2001 thanks to the anthrax attacks in the U.S.

As was later confirmed, the spores in question were actually derived from the Ames strain, a strain of anthrax used at the United States Army Medical Research Institute of Infectious Diseases. Unsurprisingly, once the anthrax was found to have sourced from the U.S. government's own biological research labs and not an Iraqi weapons program. Was this another false flag to start medical marshal law legislation?

The manipulated legal system even claims rights to inject your body with vaccines. Realize we are dealing with a sociopathic system, and do you want to be injected with an experimental vaccine, while your ability to make an informed decision is suppressed.

An informed and engaged public is far less likely to go along with wars waged for power and profit for the Elite few at tax-payers' expense — and a greater expense for the countries invaded. And, as the public becomes better informed about the very issues that the media has distorted for so long, they will realize that the answer to manipulation is to not to buy into the distorted perceptions that are sold as factual news. Instead, listen to independent reliable sources such as the Corbett Report (www.corbettreport.com). By spreading the truth, more people can awaken.

CHAPTER 2

CAPITALIZE ON THE WEAKNESSES OF CORPORATE RULE

"You assist an evil system most effectively by obeying its orders and decrees. An evil system never deserves such allegiance. Allegiance to it means partaking of the evil. A good person will resist an evil system with his or her whole soul." -- Mahatma Gandhi

Most people do not realize that their freedom is at stake. We are in danger of financial and psychological serfdom; many have been facing that danger for most of their lives. The next wave is upon us. Yet the vast majority doesn't realize that shackles are being forged. We need to motivate ourselves beyond the propaganda, delusion, and beliefs that prevent action. True awakening, even to present or future horror, leads to strategic action that deals with reality.

And it can be very disturbing when you see the global suffering the Corporate Elite cause. Despite the initial shock, it is best to be aware of the landscape, who the opposition is, and what they are capable of. The operating system was previously described with its evolution and present structure. It is a structure with inherent weaknesses that can be exploited with some simple strategies.

CHARACTER FLAWS OF CORPORATE PERSONHOOD

If we are to shift from the existing system, it is advantageous to understand the inherent weaknesses of this system that we want to change. We are confronting a hierarchical structure galvanized by international corporations, corrupt governance and black-ops. This Elite Corporate System that sustains corporate rule has strategies, structures, values and governances that are not like the way normal society runs things. It is important to understand these different rules and principles they operate by.

This is a sustained system; therefore, it has an inherent structure. Each structural element within the system of corporate rule has weaknesses. Strategies for systemic change are optimized when they address these weaknesses.

HIERARCHY

This is a structure that consolidates power and wealth at the top. A pyramid shape facilitates control by a few. Layers of empowerment and approval can make reaction and response slow. This means a quick response is needed when actions are occurring to do harm. Communicate, network and organize rapidly. It is a responsive, targeted approach like guerilla warfare used in the American Revolution, without the violence. This is achievable through well-networked grassroots organizing on a local level.

Commands and details can be short-circuited anywhere along the hierarchy chain of command. That means there have been, and will continue to be, whistle- blowers. The consequences of truth-telling have become more perilous. There have been and will continue to be whistle-blowers. As individuals start to see the big picture, and their moral compass aligns to a higher consciousness. It is important to actively support these truth-tellers. They are censoring the Internet, so there is an additional challenge to get the truth out.

The antithesis of hierarchy is grassroots-organizing and local empowerment. Organizing at the base of the pyramid facilitates a different wiring, where the power goes to the communities that generate the wealth, instead of being wired to the elite few. This rewiring is possible at the base, and is illustrated in Chapter 5.

There is a very narrow perspective, seen through the lens of self-interest and domination. Because their pyramid top is disconnected from the base, it lacks empathy. It is a cold and heartless system. That is not our deeper nature. If we have a system that embraces empathy, compassion, and community, we are creating something that aligns with a higher consciousness. This is attractive, while the nature of corporate rule with its low consciousness is repulsive.

CONSOLIDATION

The antithesis of their consolidation is spreading out over the base. Empower local businesses and ventures. Presently there is an all-out effort to destroy small and mid-size businesses with the pandemic lockdowns. It means that as consumers, we need to continue to purchase from local businesses. Now we are faced with the blowing up of our economy. The corporate elite have their plan -- to pick up the rubble, and consolidate, and profit further. Help prevent this by participating in local exchange.

By supporting local farmers' markets and swap meets, you help counter the move to wipe out small and mid-sized business. Have your town provide a place in the commons for local vendors. Utilize local exchange to bypass the mega-corporations. Local currencies work if enough of the local businesses agree to utilize them in addition to Federal Reserve fiat currency.

The shifts to support and develop local exchange can happen rapidly -- if you have the support of the majority of the governing council or board representing your local town, city or county. They have the power to change charter amendments, ordinances, and laws so they are supportive of local businesses and exchanges. This strategy will unfold in upcoming chapters. Foundational to local community business is the maintenance and development of the commons.

The commons are comprised of valuable assets that belong to all of us. This includes clean air and fresh water; parks and roads; the Internet and scientific knowledge. Public services like libraries, schools, recreation centers and public transportation. When you stop to think about it, most of the essential elements of our lives exist outside the realm of private property.

Many commons are now grossly neglected or mismanaged, because in the corporate elite systems, it's assumed that anything that does not make money is not worth caring about. That's why so many school buildings are in disrepair, and why a lot of public spaces are rundown and empty. As we support the common good, we evolve what we share in common, which at its essence is the Spirit of brotherhood and sisterhood. Now is the time for the community to reclaim our common-wealth.

The theme of spreading out and connecting on a grassroots level is about empowering the many instead of consolidating power to the few. It is nature's way to spread growth and vitality over a wide area. It is how ecosystems flourish. It helps create vibrant communities. It's not about sucking up the life force of the surroundings and dominating. This only paves the way for a barren landscape with a bleak future.

BACK-DOOR DEALS

Agreements, plans and strategies are made behind closed doors, benefiting the people and their associates behind those doors. They limit inclusion and rig everything for their own benefit. It is important to expose these scams. Especially when they hit home.

Both Democratic and Republican Party bosses, influenced and funded by big- money interests, tell elected party members how to vote and threaten them if they don't do as they are told. A Massachusetts State Representative I knew laid out the scam. When a bill or some big appropriation comes up for a vote, the chairperson or their party boss will tell them how to vote. If the boss sees they are leaning the other way, the entreaties begin. "Don't expect the party's funding to support your re-election." "We will get someone to replace you who will vote our way." Same happens in the halls of Congress and the Senate, that is buzzing with corporate lobbyists.

Acknowledge representatives who stand up to the corruption. Note who refuses to play the game and doesn't follow the party line, but instead supports the people. In turn, they should be supported by the people. This is true on federal, state, county, city and town levels.

There are often reporters who are willing to take the challenge and face the danger of truth-telling. Share their blogs and posts when they expose corruption in the government. The reliance on sharing the truth cannot be with Main Street media, but must be with grassroots, independent media and talking with friends and neighbors. We need to support reporters of truth like Julian Assange, who merely provided leaked facts to the public and has since been persecuted. What makes back- door deals work is secrecy; its enemy is exposure. Once the deals are exposed, voters can decide based on facts.

COMPARTMENTALIZE

The structure divides tasks among their minions, assuring that the Elite few understand the big picture. It takes a lot of energy to be deceptive and hide the truth. It can, and is, being done. If those who are down this hierarchical ladder don't know the big picture, the base of the pyramid is certainly not getting it.

Mainstream media reports on these compartments. They also spend much of their time reporting on diversions, half-truths, and fake news. Chopping and spinning the mainstream media provides a veil for nefarious acts, including tearing of our social fabric and their repercussions.

The big picture ties these fragmented puzzle pieces into a mosaic that educates and makes clear what has been hidden from view. That is the intention of this book. By objectively providing facts, the pieces fall into place.

Compartmentalizing opposes an inclusive approach of teamwork and transparency, both of which are inherent in grassroots organizing. One strategy of communication and empowerment is to spread them to the many; the antithesis is the present system. So, it is not empowering and informing one pyramid head, but spreading it out to the many. When the base is empowered, it thrives.

Grassroots is an approach that works. It is not about control and division; it is about empowerment and collaboration. This becomes part of a larger strategy to effectively move forward and release these shackles that are tightening their grip.

DIVISIVENESS AND SYSTEMIC RACISM

Corporate Rule uses divisiveness to help assure that the 99% does not organize. Their nature is to break up the organizing around them, to assure their domination. It involves the media stirring up emotions about immigration, religion, abortion, gay rights.

Now the divisiveness takes a new turn. Maskers vs. non-maskers, vaccines vs. non-vaccines, opposing the propaganda vs. following Corporate Rules. Anything that develops clashes among residents is a good strategy. Anything to prevent focusing on the real issues. For some, this is a wakeup call to the injustice of the system, for others, it is about doing what Uncle Sam tells them.

This divisiveness goes deep as systemic racism. It is a reflection of the very top of this pyramid hierarchy. The eugenicists' philosophy thrives among these ultra-elite. Because they have amassed tremendous wealth, they feel ordained to rule over the many. They are separate from the lower peons. This opposes home rule, where there is no discrimination. It is like an athletic team, where your ability and heart determine your contribution to the goals.

As we realize and act upon our common brotherhood and sisterhood, we acknowledge the deeper bond that unites all of humanity. It is about going beyond the external wrapping to the human being inside. When we embrace this common bond, we also bond with a more spiritual dimension that is beyond divisions.

Our nature is not about bigotry and separateness. Reflect on your own experience when you are with people you care about and the contrast that when you are isolated due to the lockdown. The harmonious human connection feeds our energy and spirit. It is our deeper nature.

LOYALTY AND SECRECY

The most important qualification of membership and rising in the system is loyalty. Participation is first built on loyalty, not competence. Members must carry out orders and must go through an arduous process of proving their allegiance through different levels as they advance in this Elite System.

Acknowledge and support whistle-blowers. If they are not loyal to the scam, they face reprisals that include torture and imprisonment. You don't have to go far to realize that the Eric Snowden case is a poster child for the extent the United States goes to punish those who disclose information about the Deep State.

When information is disclosed, save it on your PC. Information is being scrubbed from the Internet at an alarming rate. Do your best to communicate about what is happening and what we can do about it. The antithesis of secrecy is the broadcasting of truth.

This means that methods other than mainstream media must be employed.

The well-vetted internet sites like CorbettReport.com provide links to other sites that give reliable information. Provide information to your friends and acquaintances. Let people know what is under this veil of secrecy.

DARK VALUES

This includes deception, manipulation, lies, greed, theft, self-centered delusion, and even murder. Those who rise to the top have their moral compass pointed toward their profit and power. They employ evil and domination as core values.

If a person is immersed in an environment since birth, it becomes the norm. The sociopathic system is so normal, people act accordingly, thinking it is the way to advance. So those darker values and sociopathic tendencies creep in.

Most people's moral compasses won't allow them to willfully harm others for profit and domination. Our deeper nature is love and compassion. Although everyone is not coming from this deeper place, it is inside all of us. Love has the power to unite all and shed light on darkness. On an energetic level, a great power is possible through connecting in a place of love and respect, enough to overcome these dark forces.

This is not a revolution, but an evolution. If everything is energy and consciousness, then we are moving toward a higher consciousness and vibration. The highest vibration is love. It is the antithesis of the low-vibrating energy and consciousness of dark values. Corporate rule only takes humanity further from the Light. If a system is created that embraces the higher vibration, there is a shift that occurs. It is an evolutionary step, and it is our nature to evolve.

WEAPONS

Their weapons to subjugate the masses are many and keep on changing. Tactics using medical martial law, the lockdown of society, and the destruction of businesses and lives is part of the most recent wave. Our governance scripted by corporate lobbyists, election rigging, control of the higher courts. The military/industrial complex serves corporate agendas. They also use chemicals in our food and, the repercussion of glyphosates in your food will increase. They have even managed to weaponize weather with programs like HAARP. Now it is 5G radiation being forced down a community's throat when proven health risks exist, making constant surveillance possible.

An important counter weapon is truth and exposure. Do your research on the pandemic and go to www.CorbettReport.com for researched information and their sources of the actual statistics. Look into the excellent report on Bill Gates and his goal to inject the entire global population. It is much better than listening to talking heads who read a distorted script. Be aware of developments. There is coercion to take this experimental "vaccines" by potentially requiring it for travel, jobs, school, and even shopping. The vaccine does not prevent transmission. Manipulation of the monetary system and debt form a wide variety of banking scams, including attempts to make all currency digital.

Not everyone wants to look at the facts, they trust what they are told. There has been a social construct going on for generations. It is a science skillfully developed to shape your beliefs, the main battle for systemic change. A simple counter strategy is to turn off the TV. Realize that the people who are scripting the message are not communicating truth but guiding behavior.

We are presently living in a Sociopathic System. What a sociopath and a sociopathic system fear most is exposure of the truth and removal from power. A key to removing them from power is a fair democratic election.

ELECTION INTEGRITY

Voting is a foundation of democracy; however, that foundation has become cracked and fragmented, as it is run by private vendors, states and counties. The scope and pervasiveness of methods used for stealing democracy have been ramped up since the use of rigged electronic machines in the voting process. It was further boosted in June 2013 by the U.S. Supreme Court, which gutted key portions of the Voting Rights Act of 1963, setting the stage for massive disenfranchisements in the 2016 elections, which continued in 2020.

Even with mail-in ballots problems can occur with delivery, scanning and tabulating votes. The extent of voting theft is alarming. This can be remedied by making the voting process transparent. Public hand-counting of voter-marked paper ballots is one system that allows for full citizen oversight of elections. The newest reliable systems involve hand-marked paper ballots, or voting stations that produce a paper ballot checked and signed by the voter. Optical scanners read the paper record and store the full image; after that, vote totals are produced. These tallies, which can be traced to the original hand-marked ballots, provide a verifiable account of the votes.

Unfortunately, this process is used in only about 50% of the votes cast. A large number of machines record votes with no paper trail, and can be programmed remotely, or pre-programmed, to produce a desired result. Check your county for the system used.

RIGGED VOTING MACHINES

All forms of vote collection, including mail-in votes and early voting center results, are sent to the county, where they are tabulated and sent to state headquarters. Tabulators can be remotely changed, and information over the Internet can be manipulated. Fraud has been occurring on local, regional and statewide levels – and not only with rigged election machines.

Nearly all electronic devices used in election vote-gathering and counting can be pre-programmed or tampered with in order to provide a specific result. Many have back doors where number tallies can be changed by remote devices. Some contain SIM cards, where results can be manipulated by a cell phone. No transfer of data over the Internet is safe, and all can be changed before they reach their destinations. Private corporations with ties to politicians are manufacturing voting machines that are not transparent, with proprietary source codes.

Any system that breaks away from a verified paper ballot and verifiable electronic image copy should be discontinued immediately. Let us be assured that our democratic foundation of voting is not being manipulated by a foreign country. More importantly, we must scrutinize the private manufacturers and consultants of U.S. voting machines who have positioned themselves as the gatekeepers of voting integrity. Remember that the least expensive and most reliable and transparent process is simply a paper ballot that can be digitally photocopied by an off-the-shelf scanner. An important indicator if machines have been manipulated is looking at poll data. If there is a big discrepancy from vote tallies, more than 3%, raise a red flag.

In 1975, the CIA admitted to the U.S. Senate that it was engaged in 5,000 "benign" operations, which included electronic rigging of elections in the Third World. Rigged elections, however, were infinitely preferable to bloody coups, at least in the agency's estimation.

In the 1988 New Hampshire Republican primary, former CIA director George H.W. Bush trailed Bob Dole by 8 points in polls taken on Election Day. This was the first large-scale use of computer election machines. When the votes were electronically tallied, Bush beat Dole by 9 points. Mainstream election statistical analysts claim that a 17-point turnaround is a "virtual statistical impossibility."[17]

In 2016 elections, Bernie Sanders lost the Massachusetts state primary race to Hillary Clinton by 1.42%. However, out of the 351 municipalities that run elections, 68 of those locations hand-counted the vote and Sanders won that by 17.9%.

Over 5,000 subcontractors and middlemen have access to perform work on election machines for any clients. All political power can be converted over to a few anonymous subcontractors and private companies that have close ties to politicians.

For sobering insights on how easily the majority of voting machines can be manipulated remotely through central tabulator manipulations, go to BlackBoxVoting.org and watch two videos by Bev Harris: "Fraction Magic" and "Hacking Democracy."

GERRYMANDERING OR STACKING VOTER DISTRICTS

This occurs often in many states, when a political group tries to change a voting district to either create a result that helps them or that hurts the opposing group. Named after Elbridge Gerry, who rigged representational districts to favor his party in the 1790s, gerrymandering basically works by wasting votes and misrepresenting the general population by manipulating voting district lines. It creates a situation in which politicians choose the voters, instead of the voters choosing their preferred candidate.

VOTER SUPPRESSION

This occurs often with discriminatory *voter* ID laws that arose following the Supreme Court's decision to strike down Section 4 of the Voting Rights Act, which some argue amounted to voter suppression among African Americans. Voter ID laws can undermine voter turnout by several percentage points.

Another tactic is to remove voting machines in precincts that will vote against their chosen candidate. For example, in the inner city of Columbus, Ohio, in 2004, the wait times were 3-to-7 hours. Not having sufficient voting machines at targeted polling stations created lines blocks-long, to discourage voters from exercising their democratic rights. Also, elsewhere in Ohio during that same year, thousands of absentee ballots did not arrive for citizens until after Election Day. Not much has changed in 2020, where early voting began on October 6, the number of people who cast ballots in person during the first week of early voting nearly tripled compared with 2016, with 193,021 voters going to the polls compared with 64,312 four years ago. Yet fewer polling stations and the long lines continue in 2020 for Ohio. Vinton County, a white Republican bastion with a population of 13,500, have access to the same number of early voting sites as the

1.3 million residents of Franklin County, which encompasses Columbus, the state capital.

PURGING TARGETED VOTER REGISTRATIONS

This is concentrated in districts with a high percentage of African Americans and Latinos, and is a common practice used in many states to prevent people from voting. The process is simply to purge the voter registration list before an election. On Election Day, your name is not on the voters' registration list, and so you are denied a vote, or given a provisional ballot.

In the 1998 elections in Florida, 90,000 registered Florida voters were purged, far more than the 537 votes that allegedly decided the election for George W. Bush. Also, election officials later examined and counted the 175,000 "spoiled votes"; Gore would have won by 29,000 votes.

An honest vote is crucial for a peaceful transition. In some areas, it requires activism. Most US counties determine their regions' voting process. Your County Clerk can provide information on your region's vote manipulation or integrity.

THE POWER BASE

"When spider webs unite, they can tie up a lion." ~ Ethiopian proverb

Where do the Corporate Elite Systems derive their power from? The answer is from the base of the pyramid, the foundation, where the productivity, wealth, and power are derived from people who actually produce something of worth. People who do construction, health care, education, grow food, develop technology are the ones generating wealth. This power and wealth get sucked up into higher levels of superfluous management and concocted claims. The wealth gets diverted to fuel situations that hurt society and further subjugate the 99%. We live in a society that redirects these riches through the wiring of Elite Systems. Yet the true holders of power and the ability to transform the system come from the foundation where the grassroots are. Because the 99% is the power base, it holds the ultimate power control.

It is up to the citizens' collective effort to remove local corrupt good old boy networks and Corporate Elite Systems, and prevent them from continuing the terror that they have sent onto this planet. The most direct path is where we still have power, authority, and influence. We must go to the base of the hierarchy pyramid.

In the *Lord of the Rings*, when the source of power of the all-Seeing Eye was destroyed, the tower and evil collapsed. The all-seeing evil eye toppled when its power source, the ring, was destroyed. Likewise, when we stop the flow of energy to Elite Systems, it too will collapse. So, we must cut off the power from the evil overseeing us; the power switch is at the base of the pyramid.

This grassroots movement at the base of the pyramid brings with it a very advantageous set of strategy characteristics. For grassroots to be most effective, it must be non-violent, decentralized, self-propagating, liberating, inclusive, territory-capturing, adaptive, flexible, minimally confrontational, and uplifting.

Home rule systems supporting the common good are wired to spread local empowerment to the many. There is openness and collaboration, which generates a greater ownership and participation in local community development. A wide variety of organizational structures can be used to engage participation and support.

The distinctive wiring characteristic of the Elite system puts its consolidation, centralization and control of power into the hands of the few. Rewiring government and corporate control involve moving away from consolidation and hierarchy. This means going to the base and having resources more locally controlled, with transparency.

Power comes from a source, much like a plug in an electrical outlet being fed power that is transmitted over lines from its generation point. The collective personal energy and creativity of the residents make up the power generator. That power then gets sent through the transmission wiring of our societal systems. The most overarching direct wiring for administration and implementation is local governance. It impacts our daily life on county, city, town and neighborhood levels. Transforming the corrupt system starts at home.

The roughly 50% taxation that is imposed on income and purchases collectively goes into governance. This governance system regulates and shapes all other systems impacting society: medical, education, banking, businesses, etc. Although the top part of the pyramid is dependent on the lowest level, this pyramid base is self-sufficient.

This self-sufficient base is the county government, which oversees schools, registration of voters, property and local tax collection, police, courts, hospitals, roads, libraries, water, social services, parks, airports, municipal services and business regulation. Implementation of government and interface with our daily life occurs at the county level. With modern-day communications, the upper levels of implementation are not essential for survival. Yes, state and federal governments do play a role, but they are not the power source for systemic change.

Despite the post-pandemic world we live in, that attacks the very strength of community by restricting gatherings, we can prevail. That is the cohesive force the Corporate Elite System fears. Even though former methods of building community cohesion may not be available, we must find new ways of connecting. Internet, cell phone and text are the primary methods, and yes, they are being monitored. However, let's look to locations and platforms where we can gather, even if that means gatherings and connections are banned by the "authorities.

CHAPTER 3

THE TRIGGER FOR SYSTEMIC CHANGE

Any organization or system can rapidly grow and prosper by transforming a single trigger within the system that is so pivotal to success, it can cascade into improvement on many fronts that will affect growth indefinitely.

A trigger can quickly transform our governance, with the least amount of energy. The pressure point must be accessible by grassroots, and capable of transforming the entire system.

I have been describing the character and weaknesses of Corporate Rule. But a much broader perspective is needed if the trigger is to come into view.

We are dealing with a SYSTEMS ISSUE. Take a Step back and look at our Societal Systems: Medical, Education, Business, Government, Military, Media, Monetary …. These systems shape modern society and impact the well-being of the residents. The systems channel energy and determine the flow of money and power, like the circuitry of a computer operating system.

Government is the overriding system that regulates monetary, business, education, health care, law enforcement and military systems. It has a key access point, where grassroots have the advantage over big money.

FOCAL POINT FOR SYSTEMIC CHANGE

This primary access point within the overriding system is through county, city and town governments. The counties (boroughs) are a self-sufficient legal entity that forms the base of the government hierarchy. This is where people live, work and are most affected by government. The state and federal layers are dependent upon the base; however, the county is *not* dependent on the upper layers, but can function as a self-sufficient system.

Within county governance are concentrations of power where the trigger point of the system lies. Networking local progressive grassroots connections and strategically directing this community force to the trigger point will rapidly transform the entire system. The same applies to cities and towns.

The primary trigger is the "majority" of the County Board of Supervisors (the governing Council in local government). Also of importance are the sheriff, the mayor, and the prosecuting attorney.

This brings up the need for a well-networked umbrella approach. A local independent Standard Citizens Political Action Committee (PAC) in the U.S. can facilitate platform identification, candidate selection, access, support and development, and fundraise for all supported candidates. A non-partisan approach with local county grassroots control is definitely needed, as the major political parties have been hijacked by big-money interests.

It is imperative to have a "majority" of the governing councils dedicated to progressive values of serving the people and environment, instead of corporate profits.

What constitutes a majority varies from region to region. Getting a majority of progressives is best served by some version of a political action committee. It is not difficult to form, and can be started by a small, dedicated group. Each county, city or town should have a non-partisan, independently run organization that selects, develops and campaigns for these progressive candidates. This mechanism supports collaboration among county progressives and is bipartisan, independent, and owned and directed by its local creators.

A local approach has many advantages. Issues affecting your community can often stir up emotion and the need for a resolution where progressive candidates can develop their platform. It is where mainstream media have the least influence on local issues. Local independent sources of information are more easily geared for the local scene. It is the most accessible entry point, is where you live and impacts you directly.

Local citizens can develop their own political party that is not about selecting Wall Street Democrats or Republicans. The existing party system rigs it, in large part, so your selection is limited to corporate rule representatives. These political parties are Elite clubs that are not part of the federal government; they can easily dismiss legitimate candidates who support the people, like the Democrats did to Bernie Sanders, or Dennis Kucinich before him. Also, remember who controls the media.

On a county, city and town level, the citizens can be the club. Or citizen groups can gain local control of a party and select proper candidates. The "brass ring" is getting the majority of the County Council to represent the people and environment. The U.S. counties are a self-sufficient legal entity that cares for most of the commons. Other nations use names for local governance like parishes, boroughs or municipalities. We need not go any further, because this is where the real power lies in governance of communities.

UNDERSTAND THE BATTLEGROUND

County government is where the "rubber meets the road." They are the implementers, and the government layer closest to the residents. By electing a majority of Progressive seats for the county, the community will see positive near-term results. The county is the government you interact with daily. So, it is important to know the origins of counties and the power they hold.

American county governments are historically rooted in the English shire. Shires were governmental units created in the ninth century by the kingdom of England to serve as local administrative arms of the crown. The shires were renamed "counties" after the Norman Conquest in 1066, but retained their function.

For most of U.S. history, the core function of county government was to fulfill administrative mandates and carry out local tasks. These included functions such as: assessing and collecting property taxes, registering voters, administering elections, providing law enforcement, prosecuting criminals, administering a jail, recording deeds and other legal records, and maintaining roads. Highly populated counties have additional government functions, such as the administration of mass transportation, airports, water supply, sewage disposal, hospitals, building and housing codes, public housing, stadiums, recreation and cultural programs, libraries, and consumer protection. Counties have also played a major administrative role in welfare programs, and in state-mandated environmental programs. This manages much of the commons. The number of functional roles

71

that a county government assumes is highly dependent on the population of the county.

In the United States, there are 3,242 counties and county equivalents. All states except Connecticut and Rhode Island have functioning county governments. Alaska and Louisiana call their equivalent political units, boroughs and parishes, respectively. They control resources; for example, eighty percent of GDP is generated in cities. The cities have a level of control over income generated in their domain and can impact the allocation of tax revenue. In other words, the abundance generated in our nation comes from the counties, from the grassroots, from the citizens, and this is where the foundation for systemic change is best generated.

There are three basic forms of county government: the traditional commission form, the commission-administrator or manager form, and the commission or council-executive form. Regardless which form your county relies on, a county election is necessary in order to get into office. To gain a majority would require electing two Progressive candidates in some counties, and up to five in other counties. This is not an overwhelming number.

Counties are responsible for providing core services. More than 39,000 county elected officials invest $482.1 billion annually to serve 307 million county residents across the country. Counties are able to provide a vast array of services through the work of 3.3 million employees. To help with the increasing complexity of county activities and the range of responsibilities, many county boards appoint county administrators.

In our governance, we still have vestiges of democracy. Citizens can select the candidates they want to support, regardless of affiliation; it is not Democrat versus Republican or Green. The question is, who serves the people and environment the best? Who has the character we can trust? Is it people with corporate and big-money affiliations, who have a history of shady deals and greed, that you want to elect? We can elect who represents us. This needs to start at the county, city and town levels, where grassroots participation can control the local narrative, not mainstream media and big-money interests.

The battleground is in your local county elections for mayor, the majority on the County Council and other elected local representatives. This does not mean that you do not support presidential and state races; it does mean that the county, city and town races should be the main battleground, since that is where you can connect with greater grassroots involvement. Local victories are the easiest to achieve, and the most impactful to your daily life. It also allows a networked approach with other counties, to support state and federal candidates who support the Common Good.

The 99% can spend time protesting issues, or union strikes. However, those actions rarely lead to systemic change. You can protest for Black Lives Matter, for a cleaner environment, or for women's rights, but you are protesting to those who are already in power. If they are part of a corrupt system, they will not be motivated to support your cause. Why not divert the energy used to protest into electing a candidate who will support your agenda?

It starts where the 99% have a strong say. On a county level, you can interview and choose the candidate who supports actionable solutions to the local issues you care about. Candidates can be nominated who care about the common good, instead of big-money interests. This emphasizes a focus on county government, where grassroots networking can be strong, where citizens are connected to each other, where local issues can bring focus to action. In contrast, Elite Systems, where the wiring that channels resources and power goes to an elite few, is strongest at state and federal levels. The local level is where grassroots voters have the biggest advantage, and hold the ultimate power.

As a community, you have the power to purge the levels above the base of the pyramid, all the way to the top. Since power comes from the base, it must have an effective strategy to be transformed to Home Rule that serves the Common Good, where the wiring of resources and power serves the 99%.

TRIGGERING CHANGE

In many ways, the basic strategy being proposed here in this manual is what has gotten the present majorities who support big-money interests in power to state and federal levels. Supporters of Elite Systems, like the Koch Brothers, invested heavily in the grassroots, funding groups like the Tea Party. They recruited average citizens from a variety of ideological groups to their cause, which was to break up state and federal regulations that restrict corporate profits. Big-money interests exploited divisiveness, based on race and abortion. They worked side-by-side with corporate-directed workers and employees, providing real boots-on-the-ground action when enough activists weren't readily available. Unfortunately, no one would be the wiser—or even care— that these "grassroots" anti-tax groups were jointly created and funded by the world's largest private oil company and cigarette company.

They organized to create state-based anti-tax and anti-regulation movements. They stirred things up within the local communities and utilized the media to craft a perception and persona to get votes manufactured by advertising agencies and public relations firms. A campaign platform often employing fear and divisiveness was developed to stir up emotions. To maintain the Elite System, many tactics, such as campaign slogans and promises with the highest appeal to voters — (but with no intention of follow-through) — are used. Their candidates dodge the questions that show what their true intentions are. PR firms provide marketable images and masks to hide the truth of their candidates. This allowed big-money interests to control the system. Once in power, they further support legislation for big money being the primary mechanism for election success. Stack the high courts with big money supporters. This is not *real* grassroots organizing; it's more like Astro Turf!

Grassroots efforts for the common good is a very different process, with a different result. There is no reliance on big money and the channels of Elite Systems. Instead, this grassroots approach must rely on a truth that touches an emotional chord, that broadens awareness and stirs up action. It is concerned with supporting the community -- instead of profits for the 1%.

Your county, city or town can prioritize the issues and needs of the community to develop your own local political platform. The selection and nomination of candidates who support your platform is crucial. In the past, the nomination of candidates has been controlled by big money. What you end up getting is a choice among candidates, all of whom support big-money interests and agendas. Or there may be one or two grassroots candidates who support the common good, but if they are the minority, no shift for the people will happen. This can change when you select and support a majority for the County Council, Mayor and relevant county seats who are true representatives of the community and common good.

RICHMOND COUNTY, CALIFORNIA

There are counties in the United States where majorities were elected who promoted and protected the common good. In California, Richmond County clashed with Chevron. In 2014, the oil giant was campaigning for their hand-picked candidates, who supported the expansion of their refinery. Chevron, which had controlled the County Council, called "The Chevron Five." The oil giant and related corporations spent $3 million dollars on a campaign to assure that their candidates got in. Their opponents spent just $30,000. A grassroots movement selected and endorsed the candidates who supported Richmond's common good. The campaign had a core of dedicated volunteers who began door-to-door canvassing every week, well before election season, and systematically tried to reach all the networks and neighborhood councils. Phone-banking, in cooperation with the Sierra Club, began months before the election.

The efforts relied on volunteer work and communication, instead of paid campaigners. The Richmond Progressives got considerable political support because of their open and principled positions stating that corporate funding had no place in democratic politics. They refused any contributions from large corporations. The campaigns were positive and focused on real solutions. The Progressive candidates had a shared platform, including diversifying economic development, creating a Richmond Youth Core, expanding programs to solarize Richmond, developing urban agriculture, and bringing in ways of dealing with youth violence. The campaign responded as a movement, mobilizing for City Council meetings and using the public comment portion as a forum for raising the issues that were critical in the campaign. The Progressives were victorious and got a majority on the County Council! Now, Chevron pays fair taxes and stopped the expansion of the refinery, which would have increased county pollution. This majority requires ongoing work as you will see, this effort was not maintained and they lost the majority in subsequent elections.

MAUI COUNTY, HAWAII

The story of Maui County is a story line repeated in most global communities. It clearly illustrates the power of the trigger for Progressive change. It is a story showing how the power lies within the majority of the governing council or boards of towns, cities and counties. Effective strategies and processes provide a template to transform this corrupt sociopathic system in your local area.

This template is illustrated by a U.S. county that has been under the suppression of Corporate Rule for 125 years. It has a challenging culture, divided among eight ethnic groups. Out-of-county mega corporations are pouring big money in, only to extract a much greater amount. All this goes on while the residents struggle to get by. A story of suppression that has been told for generations and is still experienced now.

The underlying system and manipulation is similar in any town, city or county wired to benefit the few while disenfranchising the many. This illustration provides the premise that is so applicable today. This story applies to you, your family and friends. It applies to all local governance. This is a systemic battle that goes to the wiring of these sociopathic systems, to the core operating system and the root of the power source.

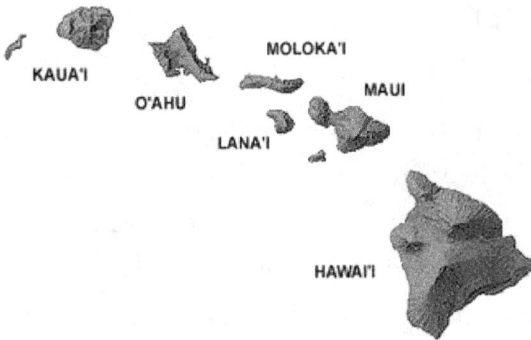

The suppression of residents, the exploitation of riches, the harm to the environment under corporate rule occurred in Maui County, Hawaii. A cluster of three inhabited islands Lana'i, Moloka'i, and Maui, in the middle of the Pacific Ocean with 168,000 residents and an average daily influx of 60,000 tourists, pre-pandemic. This tourist-based economy provided a $860 million county budget in 2019.

Our top grassroots goal was to win a majority of Progressives onto the County Council. This required winning five Council members out of the nine. They can even keep the Mayor in check. In some counties in the U.S., this ruling body consists of five or three, or even two members making a majority. Getting that majority for the County Council is the main goal which we accomplished in 2018. It is a direct path to locals gaining local power. It is the strong entry point to changing state and federal representation, as it engages grassroots in a doable way, and big money is not as empowered.

In the 2020 elections, out-of-state Super PACS wanted to elect a majority of the County Council and stop seven charter amendments to get back their Corporate Rule. The Maui Pono Network became a community hub for election information and supported 9 Progressive candidates and 7 charter amendments. The out-of-county Corporate Super PACS poured in 43 times the amount of money we had to support the exact opposite of our slate.

There is nothing like a David-and-Goliath story to illustrate how six dedicated activists provided a catalyst to defeat big-money interest. The Maui Pono Network resoundingly beat the opposition; a Progressive majority now rules. This small group helped win 6 out of the 7 charter amendments, transforming the wiring of cronyism and control. The result is a huge, positive shift despite the challenge from the pandemic having the second-largest unemployment impact of all U.S. counties, with 90% of its industry coming to a halt.

Yet this is a story of hope, and provides a clear path for towns, cities and counties to truly focus on the well-being of their residents and provide opportunities to flourish in new ways. Just the simple wiring of the tax structure for the ultra-rich to be in line with the rest of the nation allows the system to address community needs. But you need a majority that supports the community instead of the ultra-rich.

This is a doable contribution you can make to your community. It can have positive repercussions for generations. Anyone with good communication skills can take on this initiative, which can have an immediate impact, both in your neighborhood and county-wide.

The transformation starts with a few impassioned individuals focusing where the grassroots activities have the most control, at the local level. Anyone committed, with good interpersonal skills, who cares about their community, can play an effective role. With the template described here, it can take just nine months to transform your county. Citizens help to develop the platform, selecting their nominations and campaigning.

When their efforts are united with statewide counties, state elections are influenced. When enough states elect Federal Congress representation that serves the common good, federal legislation can be changed. This enhanced network can even result in a progressive White House! It is all fueled by the base of the pyramid, where the change effort needs to concentrate. It all starts by listening to your community.

CHAPTER 4

LISTEN TO THE PAST TO UNDERSTAND THE PRESENT

"There is no act too small, no act too bold. The history of social change is the history of millions of actions, small and large, coming together at critical points to create a power that governments cannot suppress." -- Howard Zinn

When we hold the intention of serving the common good and are willing to broaden our perspective of our community, we can listen receptively. When we break away from the old assumptions and beliefs, we can more clearly see the challenges, strengths, and opportunities in our community. Through understanding the past, a greater level of compassion can be stirred for the present situation. This understanding carries through to provide insights into present and future strategies for Home Rule.

LISTEN

I will tell this story from my personal view of being the founder and director of the Maui Pono Network. I lived on the island 14 years earlier, when I wrote my first book on organizational development, based on my 36 years' experience as a consultant in this field.[18] I still had many friends there and after all those years, I even kept my Hawaii mobile number, believing that I would eventually return.

When I was asked to support the Progressive movement in Maui, I had to serve in any way I could. I had previously attempted to work on systemic change on a federal and state level, only to encounter tremendous blocks and barriers. My hopes were much higher for a county approach.

I arrived in Maui in August 2017 and for the first six months I simply listened. I met with civic leaders, Progressive government officials, social service experts, environmentalists, farmers, activists, housing experts, and people who had been abused by the system. I looked into strangleholds in the county system and saw how deep the roots go.

Looking into the past provides a clear understanding of local governance, culture, and compassion for what exists today. In some counties, cultural roots go deep; wounds inflicted over a hundred years ago are still felt today. This holds true for Maui County.

THE ANCIENT CULTURE OF MAUI AND ITS OVERTHROW

Prior to the Westerners' arrival, Maui was a peaceful island under one ruling family for 250 years. An estimated 200,000-to-250,000 Hawaiians were living on the islands by the mid-1700s.[19] Some estimate as high as 650,000. It was a hierarchical system, with strict rules. Everyone was well-fed, there were few possessions, and the population prospered. The islands specialized in certain skilled trades: Maui became the chief canoe manufacturer. Their ancient religion was prominent, as well as the spirit of Aloha.

Oral tradition indicates that castaways, most likely Spanish, shipwrecked on the islands sometime between 1521 and 1530. The first trading encounters in 1788 with Europeans were with independent businessmen on ships trading goods with China. Hawaiians mostly purchased goods with foods and livestock, until the traders discovered Hawaiian sandalwood trees, which were valuable in China for incense. By the 1830s, sandalwood became so scarce that logging stopped.

Whaling ships plied the Pacific along the coast of Peru and Japan as early as 1818. Hawaii sat directly between the two. Lahaina on Maui and Honolulu on Oahu became the main Pacific ports for the north Pacific whaling fleet. Since Lahaina had no real harbor, ships anchored off Maui's southwest coast for shore leave. By 1824, more

than 100 ships visited Lahaina every year. As Hawaii's capital, it quickly drew enterprising immigrants, who opened taverns, brothels, inns, and shops. Whaling ships tended to stay several weeks rather than days, which explained complaints about drinking and prostitution in the town at that time. At its height in the 1850s, more than 400 whaling ships a year visited Lahaina.

INVASION OF DISEASES ON MAUI

When the people of Maui came into contact with diseases for which they had no immunity and no effective treatment, they began to die in vast numbers. Smallpox, measles, influenza, tuberculosis, cholera, typhus, typhoid fever and sexually transmitted diseases decimated the population. Estimates range that from 30%-to-50% of the population died within a generation. The effect was catastrophic on the population of Maui. Some estimate that 1-in-17 Native Hawaiians died within two years of the western ships' arrival. The islands' population decline was rapid from the estimated 250,000 in the 1700s to: 1831=35,062 ...1850=21,047 ...1860 =16,400 ...1878 =12,109.

Estimates of the Native Hawaiian population in Hawaii

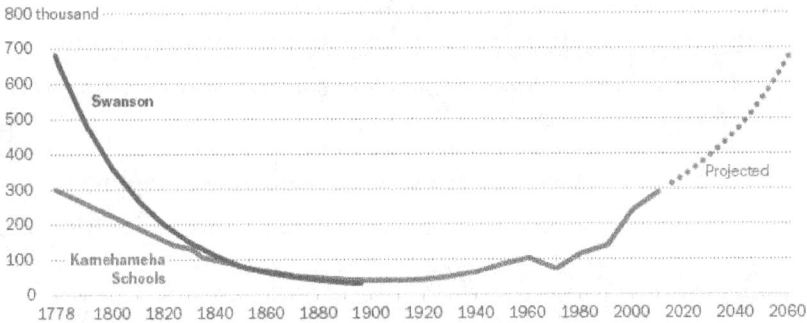

THE "BAYONET CONSTITUTION"

On January 20, 1887, the United States began leasing Pearl Harbor. Shortly afterwards, a group of mostly non-Hawaiians, calling themselves the Hawaiian Patriotic League, who were basically plantation owners and business leaders, began their takeover of Hawaii by drafting their own constitution. The "Bayonet Constitution" of 1887 was forced on King Kalakaua by the Hawaiian League, with the support of the Honolulu Rifles, a volunteer regiment. This new constitution, signed at gunpoint, severely restricted the King's authority, and disenfranchised the residents.

OVERTHROW OF HAWAII

As in the past, when power-hungry people get power, they plot to get more power. A conspiracy was hatched by Sanford Dole and big-money interests. They initiated the overthrow by organizing the Honolulu Rifles, consisting at the time of approximately 1,500 armed local (non-native) men, under their leadership. Also, U.S. Marines from the USS Boston and 162 sailors landed in Honolulu to take up positions at the U.S. Consulate, and Arion Hall, a Mormon house of worship. On the afternoon of January 16, 1893, the Rifles garrison pointed their guns and cannons across at the Iolani Palace and waited for the Queen's response.

Before any shots were fired, Queen Liliʻuokalani surrendered to avoid bloodshed due to the Queen's desire "to avoid any collision of armed forces, and perhaps the loss of life." There, she later penned the sorrowful lyric to "Aloha Oe," Hawaii's song of farewell. The overthrow left the Queen imprisoned in ʻIolani Palace under house arrest. The monarchy was dead. Corporate rule was born.

This systemic change was led by Stanford Dole, the son of American Protestant missionaries who was educated in the United States. His fellow sugar cane barons controlled all aspects of the islands' operations: banking, shipping, hardware, and every other facet of economic life on the islands. To a large degree, this shaped the future of Maui County for the next 125 years.

The island's big-money interests now forced their values on this ancient culture. The descendants of missionaries were overtaking the islands -- not in the name of Jesus, but in the name of money, greed, and lust for power. They felt entitled to steal this sovereign nation in the name of big-money interests. The new rulers blanketed the islands with their brand of wiring the system, one in which backdoor deals flourished. A system to support wealth extraction to the 1%. A system that feeds off indentured servants. A system based on racial divides and disenfranchisement of the masses. Sound familiar?

CORPORATE RULE

Entering the U.S. as a Territory in 1900, Hawaii became a plantation outpost, providing missionary-descended sugar barons and investors with huge profits. This also gave the United States a strategic military watering hole in the middle of the Pacific.

The construction of a water distribution system delivered water from East Maui's expansive watershed to the arid plains of Central Maui, and secured the future of sugar cultivation. The development of rail and ocean transportation also greatly influenced the growth of the sugar industry on Maui. Rail systems linked the fields, processing facilities, and harbor, allowing for efficient movement of sugar cane and refined sugar. Ocean transportation provided the vital connection between the islands and the world market.

Alexander & Baldwin (A&B) built one of the world's largest sugar mills in 1901 at Puunene. Another was built in Paia in 1906. The next decades brought explosive growth in the sugar industry. The HC&S Co.'s Sugar Plantation alone had 30 camps, with a total of 1,545 individual houses. Ethnic composition was Japanese (the largest group); Filipino; Chinese; Korean; Puerto Rican; Portuguese; Hawaiian; and Caucasian. Four public schools, three Japanese language schools, and ten churches were on one plantation. Recreational facilities included: a swim tank; a gymnasium, three theaters, and baseball and athletic fields.

For nearly a century, sugar was king in Hawaii, generously subsidized by the U.S. federal government. The sugar planters dominated the territory's economy, shaped its social fabric, and kept the islands in a colonial plantation era, with an organization of managers and fieldhands assuring that the incredible wealth generated would go to the 1%.

Everything of significance, from banks to shipping lines and sugar plantations to newspapers, was tightly controlled by Corporate Rule. Fully one-third of the population of the islands was living on the plantations, with 70% of the people directly dependent on plantation economy. The real power brokers after the overthrow of the monarchy and annexation were the corporations called the Big Five. Starting with the sugar plantations and branching out by means of an impressive network of interlocking directorates, they had centralized virtually all economic power into Corporate Rule. The companies, called the Big Five, were: Alexander & Baldwin, C. Brewer, Castle & Cooke, American Factors, and Theo Davies. They controlled it all.

THE DIVISIVENESS PLOY

Working the plantation fields was rigorous work for 12 hours; the pay was one dollar. Part of that dollar would go right back to the store owner, who had the only source of supplies for the plantation workers. In many cases, they would still owe the store money after all wages were taken out. Plantation owners kept selling people on big dreams, only to make them indentured servants.

Photo: H. Arango, courtesy of Alexander & Baldwin Sugar Museum

Cane Cutters and Luna Overseer, Paia, 1920s

With the decline in native Hawaiians, Chinese workers were brought in; then came successive waves of Portuguese, Japanese and Filipino workers. Each new group was used to depress the wages of the former group in the employers' insatiable quest for new sources of cheap and obedient labor. When one ethnic group went on strike, the other groups worked as strike-breakers, ultimately leading to the strike's failure. Each ethnic group occupied a separate section of a plantation camp. There was constant orchestration by the owners to prevent organizing and rile-up opposing factions.

The same holds true today. If a nation, or even a local county, starts to divide, based on ethnic, religion, gender, culture or age factors, the movement loses power and is difficult to sustain. The many agendas that form in each faction often conflict and generate competition. Republican versus Democrat, Pro Life versus Pro Choice, Immigrants versus Administrative Policy, Mask Wearers versus Non-mask. For success to happen, there must be an underlying focus that all factions can unite around. Uniting the people is the enemy of Corporate Rule.

THE STRUGGLE FOR HUMAN RIGHTS

By 1915, laws were passed to suppress organizing for justice. The labor law generally consisted of anti-picketing statutes, criminal syndicalism legislation, and ordinances restricting public assembly. Hawaii's territorial laws were the equal of any of the states in their repressive nature.

Hawaii's laborers faced almost insurmountable odds against unification and organization. Besides the autocratic control exercised by the Big Five, the labor force had been divided into opposing racial blocs.

The cultural gulf among these ethnic groups of workers was so enormous that unified action was, for many years, effectively subverted. There were Hawaiian strikes and organized Japanese and

Filipino strikes, but they all failed in the end, for the employers were organized and acted in unity, while the workers could not. With the start of World War I, supplies directed to the war effort drove up living expenses -- while wages remained the same. A large portion of the plantation workers were forced into financial destitution, which lingered after the war ended.

1920 STRIKE, FILIPINOS AND JAPANESE UNITE

After years of organizing, the Filipino Labor Union and the Federation of Japanese Labor united the Filipino and Japanese groups. The strike lasted until July 1, more than half a year, when a compromise was reached that included a 50% pay raise and more benefits. The strike had taken a toll on both sides; 1,000 strikers had gone back to work, and more than 2,000 strikebreakers were hired. The Hawaiian Sugar Plantation Association, however, lost $12,000,000 in potential income.

The Strike of 1920 frightened the political and economic power players of Hawaii. The victory brought greater restrictive laws about meeting and organizing. Trespass and criminal laws deemed almost any speech or action regarding labor as evidence of criminal intent; anti-picketing laws included a ban on union meetings. This tight net of laws, it was thought, would be sufficient to restrain labor organization.

1924 FILIPINO STRIKE AND HANAPĒPĒ MASSACRE

The Filipino strike proved legislatures wrong. Despite police repression, the Filipino workers conducted a strike that rotated through the Islands and lasted over six months. In the face of a police-enforced ban on meetings (defined as two or more workers), the sugar workers carried their strike to the deadly limits.

On September 9, 1924, outraged strikers seized two strike-breakers at Hanapēpē and prevented them from going to work. The police, armed with clubs and guns, came to union headquarters to intervene. Filipino strikers were armed only with homemade weapons and knives.

The Associated Press flashed the story of what followed across the United States in the following words: "Twenty persons dead, unnumbered injured lying in hospital, officers under orders to shoot strikers as they approached, distracted widows with children tracking from jails to hospitals and morgues in search of missing strikers."

After the massacre, police rounded up all the male protesters they could find; a total of 101 Filipino men were arrested. 76 were brought to trial, and of these, 60 received four-year jail sentences. No labor gains were made.

LONGSHOREMEN'S ASSOCIATION AND 1938 HILO MASSACRE

Hilo unionists were clearly using passive resistance in 1938. Newspaper reports of the number of demonstrators ran around 500-to-600. Protestors had all agreed to a non-violent protest, that they held to, but the police did not.

In the fray, at least 16 rounds of ammunition were fired: seven birdshot and nine buckshot. When it was over, fifty people, including two women and two children, had been shot, and at least one man was bayoneted. The savagery of the final police attacks that day is not easy to explain.

One demonstrator testified, "They shot us down like a herd of sheep. We didn't have a chance. The firing kept up for about five minutes. They just kept on pumping buckshot and bullets into our bodies. They shot men in the back as they ran. They shot men who were trying to help wounded comrades and women. They ripped their bodies with bayonets. It was just plain slaughter."

Despite the injuries, the union made no real gains. In October 1938, injured protester Kai Uratani filed a lawsuit against the officers responsible for the shooting that paralyzed him. He lost, and instead had to pay for the officers' defense costs. No compensation was given to the injured. This is the way the Big Five ruled, with their control of the system.

THE GREAT SUGAR STRIKE OF 1946

An important lesson came from the Great Sugar Strike of 1946. The sugar union sent 10 young men to a labor organizing school in California. Then, they traveled to find out what had worked and what had not. Understand the best practices of others. Build and develop what had come before. Utilize trained educators to spread the word to others. Get the entire organizing effort to integrate these best practices to optimize efforts toward change.

Another brilliant move was to connect with new workers before they landed in Hawaii and enlist them in the union. There are key circumstances for getting people on board with your platform, and these union officials did it as soon as potential union members got on-board the ships. When it was time to strike, they were prepared. Finally, after 79 days, the strike ended on November 17, 1946. With 19 cents-per-hour more (depending on paid wages), a 46-hour work week, and workers being paid in cash, the union declared victory.

THE WIRING OF MAUI COUNTY

The Democratic Revolution in Hawaii was orchestrated by Honolulu Police Department officer John A. Burns. He began campaigning to the plantation laborers, especially the Japanese Americans and Filipino-Americans he came to know while on his police beats. He began what would be known as the "Burns Machine." It is important to note that John Burns believed in grassroots organizing, and that the power of elections could overturn the corruption of the Republicans in power.

During the Burns movement, the party shifted towards egalitarianism, allowing an untapped Japanese voter base to bring them to power. Burns was accepted across ethnic divides. Again, of note is that he reached out to the disenfranchised and provided hope for change. Burns connected on the street level, and the community was inspired by his vision and what he stood for.

Three years later, in 1962, Burns won the election to become governor. Governor Burns played a leading role in stimulating the state economy and attracting foreign tourism and investment. He was re-elected in 1966 and 1970. Most in the state's large Japanese population remained loyal to Burns, who had spearheaded their rise to political power during the 1950s. Burns' running-mate in 1970, George Ariyoshi ran to succeed him as governor in 1974. Democrats have held onto a solid majority since, with near-complete control over the state's congressional delegation and its legislative and executive branches. This demonstrates the power of one person, uniting factions and empowering them through the election process.

This was one layer and one form of progressive victory. The Democratic shift happened. However, big-money interests are bipartisan. Whatever labels get you in power don't matter as long as you are in power. Over time, Republican big-money interests became Democrats. This allowed the Big Five interests to influence the Democratic Party to sustain Corporate Rule. In addition, real progressive change did not occur, as changes did not get to a deeper operating system and cultural issues. On a county level, the "good old boy network" still ruled.

Then the system shifted significantly when air travel made Maui more accessible. The Kahului Airport began commercial airline operations in June 1952. In 1966, Maui had 1,456 hotel and condo rooms, and about 189,000 tourists visited the county. Expanded flights accommodated demand. A decade later, the number of hotel and condo rooms had multiplied to more than 7,000, with more than a million visitors streaming into Maui. In the 1970s, development literally took off. Basically, the control lever shifted.

Actually, it was a simple formula to sustain the rule of the good old boy network. (1) Get the majority of the County Council on your side, so you prioritize what gets funded, who gets tax breaks, and how much is spent. (2) Have your influence with the Mayor so he is beholden to you. (3) Have key department heads be in relationship with big-money interests and implement or don't implement what the good old boy network wants.

When you take a look at the actual underlying operation, you see where "the rubber meets the road." Maui's problems escalated as county money got diverted and special deals were made: affordable housing was scarce, and residents were forced to leave their homes. Water distribution for sugar cane crops was killing off ecosystems. There were giveaways to big contractors who were part of the good old boy network. Avoiding environmental measures by big developers was common practice, while placing the burden on taxpayers. There was much illness from the toxic chemicals sprayed on Monsanto's experimental agricultural land. Sugar cane fields were poisoning residents by spraying and burning. Big tax breaks for those who had money, while the burden went to the working class.

The good old boy network continued its rule, while the vast majority of residents suffered. It was just a different form of plantation rule. There is another, deeper element that helped sustain this rule, and generated blindness to alternatives.

A CULTURE OF CRONYISM, NEPOTISM AND DIVISIONS

Since 1893, big money has ruled Maui County. This rule varied in intensity over this period and, at its worst, involved disenfranchisement of anyone outside this good old boy network. Backdoor deals were made that benefited only those behind the door.

They would get their trusted group in political power, not because of competence but because of loyalty. That way, deals could be made, and silence maintained. If you played with them, you could make your fortune, and if you decide not to, all-out efforts were made to make you fail. It was a powerful mechanism to exploit the community. In this type of wiring of the system, cronyism flourishes.

The nine Maui County Council members and the Mayor hold the power in the County Governance. Controlling these 10 positions is key. There is no election for Sheriff and Prosecuting Attorney, as they are appointed. The way the County Charter was set up, all county district seats required a countywide vote. It required a lot of backing and financial support to get elected, and eliminated many candidates who could win their district but not secure the money necessary to get enough votes countywide. So the good old boy network would invest in their candidate, who would play ball with them. Local candidates, no matter how great their credentials and record of community service, could not compete with the marketing and promotion that the opposition could afford for their candidate.

The county was structured so that the Mayor selected the county department directors, who essentially ran every aspect of the county operation. These appointments were sometimes political favors, where the appointees had zero experience in the responsibilities they controlled. Often, this resulted in the Mayor making decisions and the department head being more like an overpaid secretary. The Mayor actually coerced department heads to sign their resignation letters before they were hired. If they disobeyed him, all he had to do was accept their letter and they were out on the street -- with no recourse.

102

Selection of department heads helped assure implementation of policies supporting special interests. Those in charge were against change, because they had the system working for them and wanted to keep it that way.

There was also an unwritten policy of nepotism in Maui County government, to keep the jobs all in the family. There can be pluses in working with family members, which can support positive bonding and teamwork among workers. But when job competence is a much lower consideration than family ties for hires and promotion, the situation can become toxic. If the latter occurs, it breeds complacency in the job, a de-motivator to do good work.

Add another cultural element from the structure of the plantation camps' divisiveness. The camps were divided into ethnic groups of foreign workers for a reason. Living in separate ethnic camps with their own language, churches and stores, it was difficult to organize them. On the whole, as Maui developed, ethnic groups tended to stay in their own camps. Sections of Maui were Filipino, Japanese, Hawaiian, Hippie, Chinese, Mexican, Portuguese and transplants from the U.S. mainland; each had their own niche, and voted for their ethnic representative. So, when it came to the elections, it was more important where you were from and your ethnic ties than who and what you stood for.

Complacency and resignation set in; that's the way it is -- if you buck the system, you will pay. Whoever had and utilized the most power, authority and influence shaped the culture. In Maui County, the good old boy network shaped the culture of governance. When you are immersed in a culture, it affects your perception and subconscious beliefs. Those in a structure like this get to a place of resignation: "Things are never going to change." The Plantation Republican Party's rule set an unhealthy cultural norm that continued for another sixty years after the Democratic Revolution. That breeds a belief that helplessness; poor performance and being stuck in old ways become the norm.

There were individuals who stood out as a voice for the people and the environment. There were heroes along the way. However, when it comes to being elected to county government, the majority rules. If you only have two of the nine County Council members representing the people, big money will win out.

Divided camps need to come together to generate a unifying force, to transform the systems that rule our society. Cronyism and nepotism need to give way to transparency and competence in serving the public good. However, this situation was not in place; you could begin to see the real struggle ahead. In this culture, big-money interests were allowed to flourish and with a system and culture to keep it that way.

PROTESTING INJUSTICE

By 1970, rural Hawaiian communities were besieged by rapid development. Urbanization brought an influx of rich Americans, who, unlike tourists, actually wanted to live in Hawai'i. Evictions of Hawaiians led to increasing protest, especially in communities scheduled for residential and commercial development.

An early and typical example here was the Kalama Valley eviction on O'ahu island in 1971. Rural Hawaiians living on month-to-month leases of lands controlled by one of the largest private trusts in Hawaii, the Bishop Estate, were given one month's notice to leave the homes and farms where they had lived for more than twenty years. To add injury to that insult, these were Crown Lands, meant to serve the needs of the community. The land was leased, and the Bishop Estate had questionable ownership. Big-money interests definitely prevailed.

The residents' resistance called forth an outpouring of support throughout the archipelago. Although the residents failed to stop either their eviction or the transformation of their pig-and-vegetable farms into upper-income developments, the resistance began to spread to every island. The eventual failure of the resistance, however, illustrated the need for unity.

The sovereignty movement created a multitude of diverse groups, each having an agenda, as well as varying interpretations of Hawaiian history. This movement in Hawaii eventually expanded to become a part of the global movement of indigenous peoples. But the force and collectiveness of the voice eventually grew dimmer because of all these separate paths.

For the Hawaiians, the initial stir and surge for change has stalled and dissipated because of different agendas and claims. The battle is lost when unity is lost. Over time, different organizations with separate visions and intentions scattered the potential energy of an organized and united movement. Many Hawaiians were struggling to put food on the table, often working two jobs. They didn't have the time to address a cause that has been going on for 125 years.

Now. less than 20% of the current populations in Hawaii are native Hawaiians. If Hawaiians can unite and include all the other local ethnic groups, and stand together, that is where the power lies.

THE OHANA COALITION

In 2002, a group of progressive leaders made an attempt to shift the county power. The Ohana Coalition was used as a way to get a majority of the County Council. In this key strategy, the group conducted interviews of candidates after crafting a long list of questions. They searched for candidates who prioritized the people and environment over big-money interests, selected several county candidates and branded them the Ohana Coalition. Although they did not win a majority in the County Council, they identified the key battleground. This effort faded after several election cycles.

SHAKA AND THE GMO MORATORIUM

In 2013, two activists took up the battle to protect the health and well-being of Maui's residents. Joe Mashala and Bruce Douglas were the primary orchestrators of the GMO moratorium called the Shaka Movement, and inspired hundreds to join. Many felt it was a futile effort to go against the good old boy network directly. However, this crusade had a powerful unifying message focused on the poisoning of Maui residents by Monsanto. Joe was a passionate speaker who

maintained a positive message of hope and collaboration. They hit an emotional chord that resonated across all of Maui's diverse cultures.

Hawaii had become a dumping ground for GMO experiments and the use of untested chemicals that always accompanies them. Maui had become a testing area for their most toxic chemicals, which were not allowed on the mainland because of potential harm to the residents. Most of Monsanto's GMO testing was done to create seeds engineered to survive the application of massive amounts of Round Up and a variety of other toxic pesticides, which, of course, Monsanto also patents and sells. The main agricultural export at the time was Monsanto Round Up seed corn, used for crops throughout the U.S.

The strategies used to rally the population were simple and effective. Most importantly, many people had seen close friends succumb to cancers and experience stillbirths, and that situation was on the rise. These residents rallied; not only did they get the required signatures (9,626), but made local history by this becoming the first public initiative effort in Maui history to get on the ballot. Hundreds of volunteers worked hard to meet the daunting requirement of signatures on petitions.

Maui's 2014 GMO Moratorium also made national history. Monsanto and its agrochemical industry allies spent more money per-vote trying to defeat the initiative than any major political contest ever waged in the United States. Monsanto's team spent over $8 million, or more than $350 for each of the 22,005 votes that it received. But despite being outspent 80-to-1, Maui's grassroots initiative won by two percentage points, or 1,000 votes.

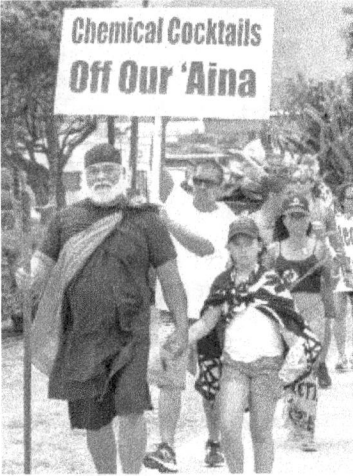

The GMO Moratorium banned the pesticide-intensive testing and cultivation of GMO crops until independent testing proved them safe, both for public health and for Maui's and Molokai's island ecosystems. Despite widely advertised propaganda claiming pesticide and GMO safety for humans, corporate-influenced federal agencies lack independent testing. Other countries have paid attention to facts from studies not sponsored by Monsanto and have eventually banned its use.

The November 4, 2014, passage of the GMO Moratorium initiative was a cause for celebration among public health and clean water advocates—locally, and around the world. It was achieved through an extraordinary collaboration between parents and residents allied with Native Hawaiians, environmentalists, water protectors, and organic farmers.

What happened after the election was even more historic than the passage of Maui's first public initiative. Maui County stands out in the textbooks of American history as the only jurisdiction ever to have the results of a legally passed public initiative nullified by federal court order; local democracy was, in fact, stolen from its voters by a corporation. This historic theft of democracy shows that our genetically modified democracy was engineered for corporate profits.

On November 13, 2014, just one day after lawyers for the GMO Moratorium requested that a state judge compel the County to enforce the terms of the voter-passed initiative, Monsanto's attorneys filed an action in federal court to grant an injunction blocking the law from taking effect. That resulted in an agreement, and a judicial order, between the Maui County Council and Monsanto to suspend the democratic will of the people until it could permanently be strangled by a higher federal court.

Here is where the alarm should go off for every citizen in the United States: **Monsanto's right to profit from its operations in Maui trumped the majority vote and right of Maui's citizens to protect their families' health and their environment.**

The federal court couched this decision in judicial parlance: that the democratic rights of the people of Maui County were "preempted" by the power of the federal government, through (lobbyist-influenced) agencies like the FDA, to regulate which products and pesticides could be used in commerce. Regardless of whether citizens were dying of cancer or watersheds were being polluted, as long as these federal regulations were followed, local government -- even though there was a passed voter initiative -- had no power to intervene or to limit the corporations' "right" to profit.

These big-money interests are also spreading an alarming amount of cancer-causing glyphosate, found in nearly all non-organic food. There are concentrations of cancer where GMO farming is concentrated. Yet politicians and judges declare that we have no rights to protect our safety, and that corporate profits are paramount, that corporations and the good old boy network have the power over the citizens. This injury and disenfranchisement reaches all parts of the United States and the globe, and is a reflection of Corporate Rule.

Now we are witnessing another level of disenfranchisement during this present crisis, and what the elite Corporate rulers are trying to force onto the public as they introduce their New World Order. We can put an end to this if we have local representation that champions residents' wellbeing and the vitality of their environment.

The 2018 election cycle was critical for Maui. The last plantation had just closed, and the future of the County was in question. It was a time of transition, and Maui needed a majority of Progressive County Council seats so that its governance served the common good instead of big-money interests. Certain charter amendments that the County Council could make would empower the voice of the people, assure transparency, and see that our resources are used wisely. With so much at stake, so community members took a different approach, an approach any community can take.

CHAPTER 5

ACHIEVING HOME RULE

"Never doubt that a small group of thoughtful, committed citizens can change the world. Indeed, it is the only thing that ever has." – Margaret Mead

STEP 1 - GET STARTED

- Listen
- Look Within
- Network

STEP 2 - BUILD A LOCAL CITIZENS' POLITICAL ACTION COMMITTEE

- Form a Steering Committee
- Build an Organizational Framework
- Create a Web and Social Media Presence
- Launch Your Local Organization

- Develop Working Committees

STEP 3 - SELECT CANDIDATES

- Identify Your Platform
- Interview Questions and Process
- Select Top Candidates
- Teamwork with Selected Candidates

STEP 4 - CAMPAIGN DEVELOPMENT

- Campaign Challenges
- Narratives and Memes
- Fundraising
- Candidate Support
- Events for Candidates

STEP 5 - LOCAL ELECTIONS

- Campaign Strategies
- Voting Integrity

STEP 6 - MOMENTUM FOR HOME RULE

- Celebrate Victories and Analyze Results
- The Challenge of Candidate Betrayal
- Support a County Progressive Liaison
- Charter Reform

The story that unfolds illustrates the trigger, the strategies and a template to gain home rule that serves the common good. This approach is reproducible for each community, town, city, and county throughout the United States. It can be used by anyone governed by an unjust hierarchical system.

The systemic transformation starts with a few impassioned individuals focusing on where the grassroots organizing has the highest impact, at the local level. Anyone committed, with good interpersonal skills, who cares about their community, can play an effective role. With the template described here, it can take just nine months to transform your region. Regardless of the level of participation, it is an important factual story on societal change.

STEP 1 - GET STARTED

LISTEN

It starts by listening to your community, and to the past that has created the present situation. Learn about major shifts and how things evolved in your county. What was successful in bringing about change, and what blocked it. Understand the lay of the land, how things are structured and whom to collaborate with.

For this Maui County initiative, the listening previously described was a crucial step in understanding its development and existing culture. This understanding influenced the priorities and development of campaign strategies, and also provided great insight on how to cultivate the community narrative, which is a vital element for winning elections. The narrative needs to align with or address the collective consciousness for that area, which is reflected in the culture.

INTERNAL REFLECTION

The transformation of the system also starts from within. Underneath all we think is all we believe. Our unconscious mind and the beliefs that shape it can alter perception, motivation and direct action.

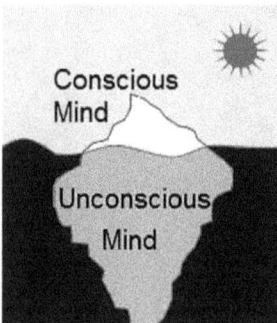

According to modern-day psychologists like Carl Jung, this unconscious layer shapes over 90% of what we perceive and, from a collective standpoint, defines our awareness of our world. Like just seeing the tip of an iceberg, 90% is submerged.

That is why mainstream media is casting its messages to shape these subconscious perceptions. It is the primary battle being waged by the elite on the U.S. population. These beliefs can be formed without our conscious mind being aware; refer to social engineering in Appendix A. The main battlefield is described in

Chapter 6. It is the biggest challenge we face. We can help change these beliefs that have been drilled into our psyche by questioning.

Question beliefs about the existing exploitive systems, an important first step toward changing our societal systems. When I questioned mainstream media's story on the 9/11/2001 terror attack, I saw the disparity with the facts and had to look deeper. Refer to Appendix B. Lifting the veil from our governance, my world view shifted dramatically, as well as my profession -- from an organization development consultant to a full-time activist.

When I observe the societal reboot happening because of a pandemic and the fear generated so people take an untested biological agent. I had to question the mainstream media story. I have to look deeper into the facts. When I see the disparity of the mainstream stories and the facts, I look at intent. Is this reboot taking us into the New World Order crafted by Corporate Rule? There are valid medical concerns regarding a vaccine that is being rushed into the blood stream of our global population. We are living in a sociopathic system; do you trust that this life-altering injection is for your benefit when it does not prevent the spread of the virus?

Question the extreme measures of Medical Marshal Law and the suppression of liberty. Question the shutdown of millions of small and midsize businesses and the picking up the rubble by mega corporations who are raking in billions of dollars in profits. Question what government, corporations and media say. Why is there a push for digital currency? What has happened to our personal privacy? What is really behind the push for 5G? Questions reveal a deeper truth and the shattering of misinformed beliefs.

Whenever we converse with anyone, it is filtered through the subconscious beliefs of both the sender and receiver. It is literally integral to our perception and ability to act. It greatly impacts our ability to develop alignment through grassroots action. It is the main battlefield.

NETWORK

I arrived in Maui in August 2017 and began listening and forming relationships. By December after lengthy discussions and an understanding of what came before, a networking strategy came into view.

Start building on what was successful. I began by working with those who developed the Ohana Coalition and the Shaka Movement building on their ideas and network. I sought advice from progressive leaders and council members. Maui Tomorrow, Sierra Club, and Akaku TV also expanded the networking. A competent core group began to form, all excited about getting a progressive majority.

An important awareness is to show respect and inclusion for those who supported initiatives for the common good and progressive candidates before you start your initiative. Ask questions, listen attentively, acknowledge their contribution. Their insight will help you avoid land mines and support your building on what has come before.

Every county has a story to tell. The listening reveals paths, strategies and who to network with. Make an effort to understand what has emerged out of the past. The insights gained still guides our actions 4 years later.

The basics of grassroots is to connect with others by listening, being open, empathizing and trying to understand their perspective, even if you disagree. Reach out to different groups.

Are there organizations that share your beliefs and vision? Take time to explore and look at gatherings and Internet events within your county. Many local groups serve community needs or are politically active. Take time to explore these volunteer programs and notice which ones resonate with your personal values and concerns. Connect around issues with networks such as fire safety groups or crime-watch. Network with a wide range of established organizations: the ACLU, Sierra Club, Progressive Democrats, clubs and associations connected with your county, and groups concerned with issues to support the common good. Utilize established grassroots connections.

Analyze the situation. Who are the elected Progressive members of your county government? Is there a group of Progressives you would like to support? Do you want to change one community issue, or do you want systemic change? If you join an existing group, go to online meetings or events. Offer to help out with something small--there's always something to be done, and no amount of help is too trivial.

Be very cautious of big-money corporate interests shrouded as the Democratic or Republican Parties. It is often best to function outside of the party system. There are exceptions if progressives have control of the local party. You want to support individuals, not institutions, with a process that is inclusive and transparent.

Connect on the Internet, attend meetings and learn about the important topics and concerns in your local area. What are the unifying initiatives: employment, medical martial law, health, financial support, food or shelter? What are your community strengths and accomplishments to build on?

Is there a local group willing to get involved with town, city or county elections? Begin with what is established and effective. If none exists, start one.

After searching Maui County for six months, I found no organization that could fit the strategic objective for the battleground chosen. In fact, throughout all of Hawaii, I could not find the vehicle needed to help assure success. There was no existing county structure that would legally allow the type of participation needed to get a majority of Progressive candidates not tied to big money in office. It became obvious that we needed an organization for the task.

STEP 2 -BUILD A LOCAL CITIZEN POLITICAL ACTION COMMITTEE

FORM A STEERING COMMITTEE

All great movements for change start with a few dedicated individuals. A small group can bring about great change locally if it has the right team chemistry and strategy. Members should share similar beliefs and vision, with good interpersonal skills.

Make sure the steering committee members are team players, responsible and listen. No big egos allowed. They must be well-respected and networked in the community. They need to possess, or have a desire to develop, certain skills to lead committees.

In Maui County, the originators and drivers of several progressive movements like the GMO Moratorium were either on the Steering Committee or were advisors for the Maui Pono Network. Some groups may begin by sponsoring an event in their area, such as a speaker or a rally. We had Earth Day Events. The expanded connections attracted by the event then added to a Progressive network directory, an important ingredient in grassroots organizing.

People were invited onto the Steering Committee based on the criteria listed and their skills. Everyone who participated were volunteers. In 2018, we had eight on our steering committee, and in 2020, we had six.

It only takes one person to disrupt this teamwork. At the beginning of our first election, we had formed a new team and discovered that one person was disruptive. We had to ask him to leave the group early on. Utilize positive and constructive feedback to acknowledge what is working, and then correct shortcomings if possible.

This core group will require a nine-month commitment prior to the general election. Your efforts can powerfully transform local governance to more fully serve the people and the environment. You can help change the systems at their root, to bring about a bright future. In perspective, nine months is a small investment in time for all the good it can do in your community for generations to come.

The process requires separate committee leaders, since these committees will operate simultaneously. All committee directors should also be on the Steering Committee and operating in harmony with all sections, to generate a symphony of activity that is well-coordinated and timed.

The director should also have expertise in that discipline; for example, the media director should have experience in web design, social media, and video production. The committees we used were:

Media, Political Platform, Candidate Selection, Community Networking, Meetings/Events, and Fundraising.

BUILD AN ORGANIZATIONAL FRAMEWORK

With the Steering Committee, clarify your vision, mission and core values. Develop a position and an intention of what you will accomplish. Your values and vision should be inspiring and engaging.

It is important to have an organization structured for the tasks required for success. A legal structure is needed where you can develop a political platform, candidate selection and campaign support. The best structure appears to be a Standard Political Action Committee (PAC) for citizens. The Campaign Spending Commission has certain requirements in Hawaii for a Standard PAC, and may vary with states. Umbrella support for Progressives, or any candidate for the Common Good, will require this type of mechanism to account for donations and campaign contributions.

It is recommended that you have the name of your organization associated with the county, city or town you are organizing for. Identify your area of focus in the name you choose. It makes your organization more relatable to the local voters, your target audience.

At the meetings with the steering committee, we brainstormed the new organization's name, mission, structure and values. "Common Good" in Hawaiian is "Pono Mau." The Hawaii State Constitution, Article 11, the "Public Trust Doctrine," describes this common good that the residents are entrusted to uphold. Pono is used in many ways on the Islands, to mean things that are right, good, balanced and correct. A wise Hawaiian elder described it as "spiritual alignment." Pono means to make things right and in balance for the people, the land, water and resources. We named the new organization the Maui Pono Network.

In Maui, the housing crisis has forced many young families off the island. So, the pleas of grandmothers, to be with their grandkids, points to the politicians who have done nothing to remedy the situation. Family, called Ohana, is a deep cultural value. All the candidates we support are for workforce housing and making housing affordable for families. So, we branded our candidate slate, "Maui Ohana Candidates."

We next consulted with our larger network, which included social and environmental groups, and social media. This allowed us to get input on our name, mission, core values and strategy. The organization and strategic plan were coming into view.

The Maui Pono Network

Our Mission: Empowering community action in the spirit of Aloha for the common good of the 'Aina (environment) and all People.

Strategic Vision

Support and elect representatives who serve the common good. It is a vital time to shift Maui from plantation-era, big-money interests to Progressive leadership for the people and the 'Aina.

By changing the system, we will eliminate major blocks to affordable housing, raising the minimum wage, sustainable development, producing abundant nutritious food, and reclaiming and restoring the land and diversifying the income base. The Maui Pono Network is dedicated to this transition.

Goals

- Develop a political platform with the County's most important unmet needs.
- Solicit, identify and interview viable candidates who support the people and environment.
- Ensure that the majority of elected Maui County Government seats are filled by the Ohana Candidates who will support the common good.
- Increase voter registration and absentee ballot use, and provide information about the Ohana Candidates countywide.
- Help change the County Charter, with amendments to end cronyism in Maui's governance.
- Develop a community network and membership.
- Create media and social media campaigns with video, memes, promotional features, and an informative website.

Core Values

- Aloha   and   Pono

CREATE A WEB AND SOCIAL MEDIA PRESENCE

Our Steering Committee co-created the organization's image. This creative process is a good team-building exercise. This group must function as a cohesive team if you are to be successful. Create a logo and design that expresses your values and mission.

Develop a consistent look and layout that can be recognized. You are creating a brand. It is a look that identifies you and provides distinction from the clutter.

Pre-launch, we also developed 30-second and 2-minute video spots describing the need for a Progressive county council majority and our vision. We also conducted TV interviews that were shown on the local community station.

Build the website as a local information hub. Focus on local county, city and town-elected offices. Let your identity be with local politics up to the county level, and post relevant news. Our site included: a means to sign up for each committee, and it was also a hub for volunteers, local issues and candidates.

Network, and compile a mailing list from a wide variety of county groups. We got on social media and connected with other online communities. Check out our site, as it changes frequently, based on community needs and the election cycle. www.MauiPonoNetwork.org.

LAUNCH YOUR ORGANIZATION

Despite the very different restrictions for contacting volunteers and voters while comparing 2018 and 2020 elections, the steps were similar. We just emphasized different strategies along the way. So, don't feel discouraged by the restrictions and lockdowns. Like the Hawaiian union members who faced restrictive laws, we too must find creative ways to connect.

Community participation was vital for success in 2018, as we focused on personal contacts to win votes. That was our successful plan, utilizing informed volunteers. In 2020, we focused on digital communication and creative ways of informing voters. The combination of the two is optimal when possible.

Announcing the Launch
of the
Maui Pono Network
"Empowering community action
in service to the common good"
Monday, March 19, 7pm-9pm
Ahimsa Sanctuary Farm, 4505 Hana Hwy, Haiku

Preparation for the launch started in early February. Setting the stage was very important, as we lined up speakers, sent announcements to potential candidates, and identified our operating committees. For one month prior to the event, we began using emails, social media, and posters to announce the meeting to the public. In March, we launched the Maui Pono Network. We only had six months until the Primary elections, with the final election on November 6.

The launch was on March 19, 2018. The night of the event was beautiful, as the moon appeared like a thin crescent in the clear sky. People were filing in as musicians played. The buzz and excited conversations made the space alive with anticipation. It was a large, open room with big windows and a deck overlooking the ocean. The space was beautifully adorned with sacred statues and quartz crystals. Some crystals were huge, 4 feet by 3 feet. The energy kept on building as 140 activists eventually filled the space.

The intention was not only to announce the launch of the Maui Pono Network, but also to inspire and recruit volunteers who wanted to see a Progressive majority represent them in county government. It was an eight-month project, and we needed inspiration. We had three existing Progressive council members as our speakers. Alika Atay, a

Hawaiian farmer-turned-activist and now a Council member, was the main speaker. He was the strong and persistent voice in the county for a Progressive majority on the County Council.

Alika opened the meeting with a Pule, a Hawaiian blessing before an event starts. He asked that all the windows and doors be wide open. In a powerful voice, he called to the Ancient Ones, Hawaiian ancestors and residents from the past who made this county their home. As he invoked their presence and blessings, a gentle breeze swept in. I got "chicken skin" all over my body as I felt a presence flooding the room. Alika asked for the blessings of the elders, and in my heart, I felt a support beyond my understanding.

The three seated Progressive County Council members spoke of the divisiveness and manipulation that is part of the present system in Maui County. They acknowledged the struggle of going against the "good old boy network," GOBN, without having a Progressive majority, and shared the frustration they experienced through gridlock and their inability to effectively serve the residents' needs. The three asked all present to participate in helping to get a majority on the Council. If successful, we would change the control of GOBN and the future of the island for generations to come! Alika and the others inspired all present to take up this community challenge, it was invigorating.

As facilitator of the event, I next asked all those present who had registered as a candidate in the 2018 county election to come up and introduce themselves to the assembly. I was amazed to see 23 candidates who were running for county offices come to the stage and announce their candidacy. The energy kept on building in the room, as people saw the need for a Progressive majority, the quality of people we could support, and what a huge difference it would make for our community.

The launch--whether virtual or in person--is important. Make your organization known county-wide. Build the promotion right up until the event through public service announcements and social media blasts. Use posters and hand out cards. Have a celebrity musician or a like-minded politician be a draw. Influence Progressive candidates to attend, and relevant speakers to inspire those attending.

DEVELOP WORKING COMMITTEES (SOCIAL GATHERING WHEN PERMISSIBLE)

Our Steering Committee wanted to assure we engaged and utilized the great energy of the launch and built on the momentum that had started. We divided the tasks that lay ahead into six action committees. At the initial meeting each committee had sub-tasks, which allowed us to display all the major responsibilities required over the next 8 months.

- Media: *Social Media, Writers, Camera, Editing, Design, Web Design*
- Political Platform: *Research, Platform Issues, Handouts*
- Candidate Selection Committee: *Background Researchers, Interviewers*
- Community Networking: *Voter Registration/Tabling, Canvassing, Phone Bank, Cross-Culture*

- Meetings/Events: *Event Support, Pot-Luck, Meet + Greet, Training for Activists, Nurturing Volunteers*
- Fundraising: *Internet Fundraising, Personal Connections, Grants*

The committee heads were gathered at flip charts spaced throughout the room. Then, each committee head described the tasks and what type of participation was needed. Participants asked questions of the committee head and then filled in a registration card for that task, if interested.

By the end of the meeting, 98 people signed up for the committees and tasks they would be involved with. We were ready to hit the road running! But we had no time to waste, as the voter registration deadline for the primary race was only a month away, and we had much to do to get our platform and candidate selection process underway. This is an important event for enlisting volunteers. Solicit people on the live Internet to sign up on your website. The following week, we started our committee meetings.

Be sure volunteers have a full schedule of activities, once you get the general public involved. Have committee meetings one week after the initial launch. Keep the momentum going. Make the meetings informative, proactive and inclusive. Since you want to develop a community, start the committee meetings with a potluck meal, if in person. Virtual makes it much easier to meet. If possible, a combination of the two works well.

STEP 3 - SELECT CANDIDATES

IDENTIFY YOUR PLATFORM

Your platform is what you stand for, what you see as important. It creates distinctions among candidates and needs to be factual. Have your Political Platform Committee conduct research on the important local issues. What are the major concerns in your county? Are there simple, proven solutions? Who are the politicians who stand against getting this resolved? What are some of the realistic solutions the county could undertake?

Through understanding the community issues, priorities, impacts and potential resolutions, you can craft proper questions for candidates you interview. Also, this is an important educational tool for candidates you select, and for the general public as you campaign. It is, ultimately, the platform your organization will stand on.

In Maui County, the platform committee in 2018 consisted of fourteen volunteers who identified the most important issues affecting the residents, visitors and environment in Maui County. The understanding by the platform committee provided the insight to ask candidates how they would prioritize and resolve these issues.

Our Committee held regular meetings to flush out the key unmet needs, how long had they existed, and why had they not been resolved before. The top local issues were identified, and the results of that work laid out our focus for what we wanted the candidates to help resolve. This information was used in several ways throughout the campaign, including candidate training, positioning/branding, narrative development, community education, and distinction of candidates.

In 2018, our top issues were affordable housing, a shift from tourism marketing to tourism management, illegal give-away to developers, food security. In 2020, the top issues were the pandemic impact, health and the community reset, affordable housing, food security and water rights.

For most communities, the top issue is the "great reset" -- coined by mainstream media. Why not reset for the Common Good instead of their Corporate Rule agenda? Do we really want a New World Order immersed in a sociopathic system? How will we recreate our community, now that our economy and businesses are in a tailspin? Imagine that 90% of the economy in Maui is based on tourism that came to a sudden halt and is slowly recovering. This is providing a great opportunity for systemic change. But this peaceful reset for the common good and home rule is only possible when you have the majority of the governing council or boards in towns, cities and counties to support this local change. For your own county, have a team identify and prioritize needs. It can be tough to look at needs that seem overwhelming, as you see businesses closing, unemployment, drug abuse, crime, hunger and malnutrition, pollution, and affordable housing scarcity. However, if you act locally, with county support, you can bring about real change. These are the important issues for your local community, and it goes to where you live.

Exploring community needs can take several forms, including available local statistics and reports, interviews, and surveys. Access to the Internet, will make this initial exploration much easier. Find community-wide statistics on overall needs comparing job development, food support, drug abuse, foreclosures, homelessness, environmental issues, public transportation, education, domestic violence, affordable housing, gang violence, teen pregnancy... the list can go on. Each town and city should have a planning department or education department where local data can be accessed. If there are no available sources that describe prioritized community needs, then find out by asking neighbors, caucuses and non-profits serving social needs.

These needs can be translated into story-based strategies that can shape public opinion. The issues can be illustrated by personal stories that evoke emotions. Emotions penetrate to the subconscious, which is the main battle. If you are in Flint, Michigan, you have contaminated water and the illnesses it has caused. Telling the story is a way to get the county officials who have done nothing out of office. It takes organizing and hitting the powerful emotional chord.

Now we have the post-pandemic reset. Past issues are still relevant, but forcing citizens to lock down, shutting down businesses and schools, and tearing the social fabric opens a new set of possibilities. To reset for the common good.

INTERVIEW QUESTIONS AND PROCESS

You must do your due diligence on the candidates. Your organization's reputation and your success in getting a majority depends on it. As a Citizens' Standard PAC with proactive members involved in county politics, you have amassed power with your growing network, both the power to invite candidates to interview, and the power of the endorsement, with a proactive plan for support.

The Maui Pono Network interviewed 42 candidates in 2018, and 33 in 2020. It requires digging into each candidate's past to understand their personal platform and past civic engagement. Look into police records and past employment of each candidate. Are there skeletons in their closets?

We had 52 questions to choose from. Have several consistent questions for all candidates. Your questionnaire should involve each of your platform issues. Interview all candidates for county offices so you know where all candidates stand. It is a way to objectively put out the information to the community so they can decide.

Our first interviews in 2018 involved renting a public space, scheduling candidates and interviews, having people travel from throughout Maui County. We did not record upon the candidate's request. After the interview, the committee debriefed among themselves and graded the candidate.

In 2020, a much better process arose through the internet. We used Zoom as our platform. We had the top Progressive leaders and activists on the evaluation panel help develop questions. Each interview lasted about one hour. During the live broadcast on Facebook, we had up to 2,200 viewers. These tapes were also played repeatedly on Akaku, our local community TV station. They were posted on our website, which had 128,000 views in 2020 as it became a hub of candidate and issue information.

SELECT TOP CANDIDATES

For several County seats, we felt that the existing candidates did not meet our criteria, so we began a search. We had several people scouring the county to help assure we were selecting the best representation. I personally asked six people to run for office. This proactive approach is part of our due diligence to assure the County was getting the best candidates. If no one is suitable, proactively conduct a search well before the candidate registration deadline. The citizens are able to choose their candidates instead of big-money interests.

A countywide grassroots effort is separate from party affiliations; in that you are essentially creating your own political party. Support the best candidate, regardless if he or she is Democrat, Republican, Green, Independent, Socialist or Progressive. You are not, after all, selecting candidates based on labels. It is the person's skill, integrity and commitment to the Common Good that needs to be considered.

In Maui County, the races for the Mayor and County Council are non-partisan. That became a non-issue. The State Representative race is partisan. We interviewed all candidates and selected the top ones.

Our evaluation included the development of a report card on the 10 most important votes made within the County Council election cycle. The depiction of the data was a hit in our community.

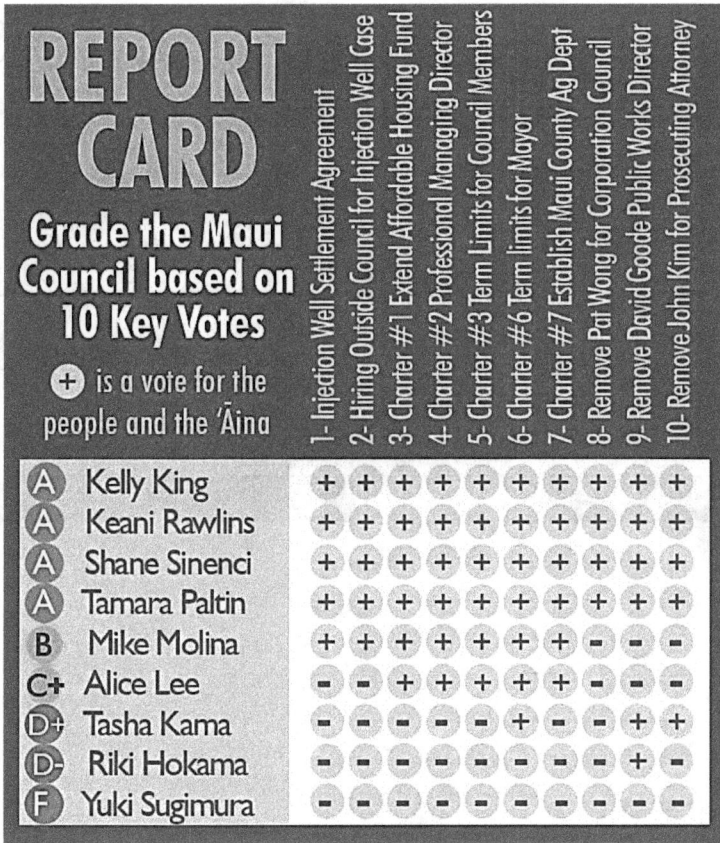

REPORT CARD

Grade the Maui Council based on 10 Key Votes

⊕ is a vote for the people and the 'Āina

		1- Injection Well Settlement Agreement	2- Hiring Outside Council for Injection Well Case	3- Charter #1 Extend Affordable Housing Fund	4- Charter #2 Professional Managing Director	5- Charter #3 Term Limits for Council Members	6- Charter #6 Term limits for Mayor	7- Charter #7 Establish Maui County Ag Dept	8- Remove Pat Wong for Corporation Council	9- Remove David Goode Public Works Director	10- Remove John Kim for Prosecuting Attorney
A	Kelly King	+	+	+	+	+	+	+	+	+	+
A	Keani Rawlins	+	+	+	+	+	+	+	+	+	+
A	Shane Sinenci	+	+	+	+	+	+	+	+	+	+
A	Tamara Paltin	+	+	+	+	+	+	+	+	+	+
B	Mike Molina	+	+	+	+	+	+	+	−	−	−
C+	Alice Lee	−	−	+	+	+	+	+	−	−	−
D+	Tasha Kama	−	−	−	−	−	+	−	−	+	+
D-	Riki Hokama	−	−	−	−	−	−	−	−	+	−
F	Yuki Sugimura	−	−	−	−	−	−	−	−	−	−

All the A's were incumbent Ohana Candidates. A panel of Progressive Leaders selected 5 State Representatives and 7 County Council candidates who represent the vision and strategy for a bright future during this community reset. Our team spent a combined 3,000 hours for the interviews, selection, and production. The 2020 Ohana Candidates the Maui Pono Network supported:

STEP 4 - CAMPAIGN DEVELOPMENT

CAMPAIGN CHALLENGES

The opposition has big money fueling their campaign. The Ohana Candidates have facts, grassroots volunteers and the promise of a bright future. By the end of June 2018, the Maui Pono Network had grown to 265 volunteers, who were enthusiastically supporting all fifteen Ohana Candidates. In 2020, we were effective with 30 volunteers. Regardless of the number of volunteers or the Pandemic, the following challenges remain.

Name Recognition: Only four of the fifteen candidates we were supporting were in political office. Eleven had no previous experience in government, and so name recognition was very low in 2018. The opposition was deeply rooted in the GOBN political machines and not only the existing candidates, but many others had parents who were part of this political stance they had held for generations. This generational political stance was part of the accepted nepotism within county government. The majority of the 166,000 residents knew the names of these opposing candidates. Ties shared, in some cases, were very strong, and people supported the candidates regardless of their voting record. Basically, we had a slate of mostly unknowns, compared to the opposition.

In 2020, the lack of personal canvassing was a big disadvantage when opposing entrenched incumbents. Personal contact is tops in getting name recognition. Canvassing door to door and follow-ups are great vote-getters. Meet and Greets at different location is another campaign priority. Personal contact and follow-ups are the main recognition tool to be used whenever possible. Phone canvassing and personal appearances on internet programs and local TV grew in importance.

Lack of Funds: The Ohana Candidates were chosen based on their prior civic service, dedication to the county and its needs, moral character and not having big-money interest ties. Money was not part of the equation in their selection, yet considerable money was required to promote them in countywide elections because of their lack of name recognition. They did not have wealthy backers, and the campaign spending commission limited per-person donations to $1,000 per election cycle. Their supporters included many people who were abused by the present system and were struggling to put food on the table.

This type of scenario is repeated as counties throughout the U.S. seek representation for the 99% and the environment, which often is not backed by big-money interests. People with great credentials are energetic, have the right personality, and are passionate about making changes, but lack the financial and grassroots backing.

Keani Rawlins-Fernandez is a good example; she was running for a County Council seat in 2018 from the island of Molokai. She worked for the Hawaiian public charter school and various nonprofits that serve the Native Hawaiian community. Then she decided to pursue a dual MBA and law degree education program. Keani received a law degree, with certificates in Native Hawaiian Law and Environmental Law; and also a Master's Degree in Business Administration. Her experience at the Hawaii State Legislature included an internship as Legislative Aide that equipped her to collaborate with State officials regarding County-specific issues. She worked for mayoral candidate and Council member Elle Cochran, and has a good understanding of Council operations, as well as insights and ideas on how it can be improved to better serve the people. Yet without ample support, her odds of getting in go way down, despite her background.

Her election in 2018 underlines how crucial this volunteer networked approach is. As the youngest to take office, she has become a star in the County Council. She is chair of the finance committee and vice-chair for the Council.

County-Wide Race: The County Council and mayoral race involved all 9 county districts casting votes for all of these candidates. In most counties throughout the U.S., races and ballots are confined to the districts that the county seat represents. Here, their race encompassed three islands. That meant that a candidate had to solicit the entire county instead of one of the nine districts. Low-cost strategies like canvassing and personal relationships were limited in the scope required. More costly TV, radio and newspaper ads, and also a heavy emphasis on social media, was a drop in the bucket for big-money interests, compared to their return on investment. In the 2020 elections, they spent 43 times our budget. Truth can override propaganda, but you need to organize.

Ethnic Divisiveness: Ethnic diversity can be a collaborative creative exchange of cultures and ideas. Or it can be divisive. It can separate people in camps, opposing each other, or looking at each other as inferior. In Maui, it was politically divisive; for example, the Filipinos would canvass and sign-wave for the Filipino candidate. Their family clans would vote for their candidate's ethnic connection, regardless of their affiliation with big money. So, the Japanese and Hawaiians had their own camps, where ethnicity was more important than the candidate's ties with the good old boy network. A simple solution is to have a diverse group of candidates you are supporting. In 2020 for the general election, 6 of the 9 candidates were women, and included Hawaiian, Portuguese, and Japanese.

Don't Confront: Maui's culture is somewhat unique, with its heritage of Aloha that influenced the residents' behavior. You can refer to it as a collective consciousness. This held true especially for residents over 50, who made up the vast majority of voters. The belief was that confronting someone or attacking someone is a great offense, no matter what they have done in the past. If you confront them in the present, you are the one frowned upon. So, candidates couldn't really confront the opposition's affiliation with GOBN or past shady dealings; otherwise, it would backfire. The debates were structured so as not to confront candidates about past records, but to paint a rosy picture of their future on paper, which disintegrates in 6 months.

The Maui Pono Network's role is to educate residents so they can make informed voting decisions. We became the conduit for showing points of opposition and the facts backing them up. So we made memes and targeted mailings.

Upcountry - Who Represents YOUR Values for House Rep?

Simon Russell
'Aina Advocate

= or =

Kyle Yamashita
Corporate Advocate

Simon supports organic farming and is a sustainable and regenerative family farmer and advocate.

Simon's campaign funding is almost all Maui funded with zero corporate dollars and he is a champion of grassroots causes.

Simon supports affordable housing for Maui's kama'aina.

Simon flew to Oahu 21 times to oppose HB 1326, the "Water Theft Bill." Simon supports local control of our Wai and watershed resources through creation of a "Maui Water Authority."

Kyle promotes GMO farming and has taken $24,000 from GMO, Monsanto and tobacco interest.

Kyle's Campaigns have been 86% funded by mainland and off island contributions of $430,000 - heavily funded by corporations.

Kyle supported airport parking for tourist cars for $340 million.

Kyle supports foreign corporate control of water and voted yes on HB1326, which if passed would have granted control of East Maui water resources for 10 years to a Canadian pension fund and A&B.

Simon Russell, raised in Hawaii, is an organic farmer and lives upcountry with his wife and children. Simon has been a been a longtime advocate for Maui farmers, families, and natural resources. He is a living example of aloha 'aina in action, serving our community and helping us protect and preserve the 'aina for current and future generations.   More info: Russell2020.org

Voting and Same Day Voter Registration at Wailuku Community Center: July 27-Aug 7, 8am-4:30pm and Sat, Aug 8, 7am-7pm.
This mailer produced and paid for by: www.MauiPonoNetwork.org Get Involved. Volunteer. Donate.

Campaign Managers: Although the Maui Pono Network served as an umbrella supporting 15 candidates, each candidate had their own campaign manager in 2018. Only one manager was a Professional. They were, for the most part, well-meaning volunteers. One campaign manager represented two candidates, who seemed to sabotage things and disengaged from collaboration. As time went on, most of us were convinced he was a plant to bring down the candidates, which he did. That was a lesson we took to heart in 2020 and worked closely with all the campaign teams.

Hawaiian Disconnect: The Hawaiians, as well as other ethnic groups, had felt the scourge of GOBN for 125 years. If you speak up and go against GOBN, you suffer consequences. There have been attempts for generations to change the system, only to see nothing significant change, so why bother? Also, many who believe in the separatist movement feel that if they vote, even now, they will legitimize the takeover of 1893. So, they refuse to participate in any elections. This is an ancient culture of the Kapu system. If your chief

143

says we go to war, you comply. You don't disobey the rules for fear of death. So, when the old Hawaiian chiefs say vote, a large number of Hawaiians will participate in elections.

Mainland Whites: If you are not born in Hawaii, you are looked at with great suspicion. Their history shows mainland whites doing great harm. I am white, born in Rhode Island, was back on the island for less than a year and became the director of the Maui Pono Network. This was initially used against us in the newspaper, and on the Internet.

We had to address each of these challenges. For example, for this "mainland white" issue, people saw that 10 of the 15 Ohana Candidates were Hawaiians and 9 of the 15 were women. We always featured the candidates and respected local Hawaiian activists. I had a low profile because it was all about featuring and supporting the candidates in their election. My background of 33 years in organizational development at the time and being author of a grassroots guide gave my presence validity. After a short time, that criticism against me died away. Each issue was addressed in the campaign strategies.

NARRATIVE AND MEMES

A social movement for systemic change tells a new story. That means building a narrative on facts and experience that evoke emotion. It may be the opposite of what big-money spokespersons are saying, or the corporate media. We must reframe the debate by telling a story that wins public support. Shaping the community narrative is an important battle to win.

The narrative is foundational for a Progressive majority and issues that lead to systemic change. Images with facts or that depict a story are impactful. A single widely viewed image can carry a new story, and shift the entire emotional landscape. This can bring dramatic change to public opinion. The Maui County Charter Amendments were crucial for systemic change of the dysfunctional county wiring. Here are some of the memes we used to support the six charter amendments that past.

YES! FOOD SECURITY

YES! HELP OUR SMALL FARMERS GROW

YES! DEPARTMENT OF AGRICULTURE
www.MauiPonoNetwork.com

MORE FUNDS FOR HOUSING — INCREASE AFFORDABLE HOUSING OPTIONS FOR OUR LOCAL RESIDENTS

CHARTER AMENDMENT #1 2020 MAUI COUNTY BALLOT
VOTE YES ✓ ON ALL 7 MAUI CHARTER AMENDMENTS
For more information and to get involved please visit MauiPonoNetwork.com

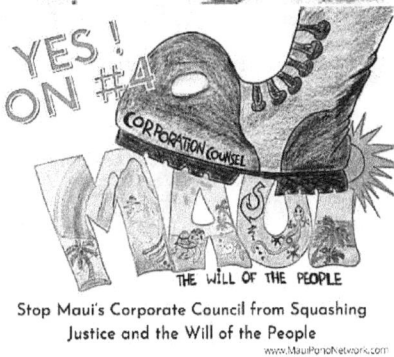

YES! ON #4

CORPORATION COUNSEL

MAUI

THE WILL OF THE PEOPLE

Stop Maui's Corporate Council from Squashing Justice and the Will of the People
www.MauiPonoNetwork.com

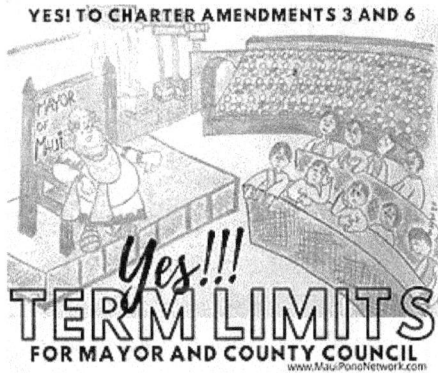

YES! TO CHARTER AMENDMENTS 3 AND 6

Yes!!! TERM LIMITS

FOR MAYOR AND COUNTY COUNCIL
www.MauiPonoNetwork.com

Candidates bring their personal story, which could include personal transformation, service, or vision. The struggles of others as a result of decisions made by elected officials is yet another story. Scams and their impact provide a perspective. Your movement for the Common Good in your region tells a particular story. The chosen stories are an effective tool when people can identify with them.

The identity is generated from a compelling story that deeply touches an emotional chord. That is when it penetrates to the subconscious, where the primary battle is. Each county needs to develop a story of the candidates, the platform issues, and what victory would mean to your local area.

Truth and community are our biggest weapons, and our subconscious is the main battlefield. Progressive organizations also need to use the same science of Social Engineering that the Corporate Elite System use to put out their propaganda. Instead of distortion and hiding facts, we went after transparency and stating the facts. Since our subconscious belief is the battlefield, repetition of the message is important. That includes sign-waving, banners, social media, newspaper, and radio.

Develop a meme that encapsulates the story. A single widely viewed image or phrase can carry a new story and shift the entire emotional landscape of an issue, leading to a dramatic change in public opinion and policy. "Occupy Wall Street" or the "99% versus the 1%" tells a story. (Refer to *"Re: Imaging Change"* by P. Reinsborough and J. Smucker.) [20]

In Maui, the position of Ohana Candidates versus big-money interests was an important story and a powerful position. For the 2020 Elections for the State Representatives for Maui County the most significant issue after the pandemic was water rights. This issue provided a clear distinction between candidates. We utilized the facts of the oppositions' votes on water legislation to show why it was important to remove these candidates on this emotional issue. We also drew attention to the impact this water policy has on the community.

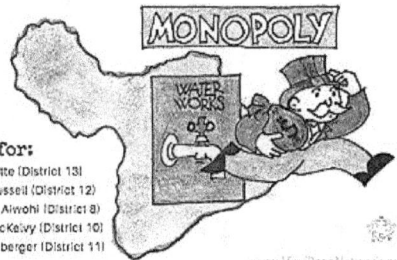

Follow the Money

NEVADA

Don't Let Off-Shore SuperPACs Control Maui's Elections

CHARTER AMENDMENTS — MAUI COUNTY COUNCIL

VOTE YES!

on ALL 7 Charter Amendments and for ALL 7 'Ohana Candidates

www.MauiPonoNetwork.com

When dark money started pouring in from Nevada to support the exact opposite of the Maui Pono Network, it was a modern-day "coup" attempt. From the previous chapter, you can imagine what this evoked. And that's what was happening when they poured $430,000 in during the last 6 weeks of the county election. As soon as we got wind of it, we immediately made three-minute videos linking it to the 1893 coup. It was shown on our community TV station ten times a day, on each of the three stations. Now that helped to stir up emotion and got people to vote. We also used memes to bring home the message.

Be an Informed Maui Voter

Vote for a BRIGHT Maui County Future

Get the FACTS at MauiPono Network. com

We knew we were having success when articles, and social media from other sources were repeating our message. Be at the forefront of the community's awareness throughout the campaign. You need an effective mechanism to expose candidate

148

voting records, funding, affiliations, involvement in private deals and interests. Informative simple messages on amendments or bills can go viral. Provide well-vetted, engaging information to educate the community. These facts fueled the community conversation. We encouraged people to blast out the information on social media and write Letters to the Editor of the local newspaper. These vital facts go far beyond campaign rhetoric, false promises, and hidden agendas.

Utilize the research on platform issues to paint a positive vision of what would happen within your region once these proposed measures are implemented. Be clear why this is important. Pass out information at all events to show what a vote for your candidates can do to enhance local citizens' lives.

FUND-RAISING

There are a wide variety of fund-raising tools for the Internet and social media. At a minimum, you should have a donation link through Pay Pal or another mechanism on your website.

A campaign that is volunteer-driven greatly reduces the money required for success. Also, an umbrella approach, supporting many candidates, is very cost-effective. However, there still will be expenses.

Prepare a budget with a list of expenditures, such as candidate cards, mailers, banners, event space, and social media boosts. There are many campaign options, and later, we will review the most cost-effective ones. Be transparent, show how the money is to be used in your donation literature.

Standard PAC rules require filing and accounting for all donations and expenditures above $25; the rules may vary from state to state. Funding limitations are a maximum of $1,000 per person, per election cycle. Primaries and general elections are two separate cycles. In Hawaii, we are limited to spending $2,000 per election for each County Council and state representative candidate. For 2020, the maximum we could spend on in-kind donations was $21,000.

The Maui Pono Network's policy is that all of the staff are volunteers. Some staff have a sponsor who helps cover their living expenses, but that is separate from the organization. All the money received by the organization goes directly to the candidates as in-kind donations. This makes it simple and easy for donors to justify their contribution.

Because of the limitations in expenditures, we do not send out big countywide mailings at a cost of $18,000. Instead, we let other local Progressive Super PACs handle big items, as that is out of our spending range. What we do is work as teams with candidates, network, and organize so we affect the community narrative. We are responsive and, on the ground, like guerrilla warfare.

Although mailers, TV, and newspapers are effective, they are expensive. It is much more cost-effective to use the limited funds for door-to-door canvassing, phone canvassing, meet-and-greets, Zoom meetings, special events, and creative signs and banners. A big hit was door hanger packets of election information. Having a well-networked social media and good relations with progressive organizations provides volunteers and donations. The more personal and in the voter's presence, the better. These are also the least expensive approaches. They do, however, require organizing and volunteer engagement.

Be aware of accounting requirements, record-keeping and reporting for your state Elections Commission. The reporting includes how paid ads, cards, and event costs are divided among all the candidates you are supporting. The accounting process should be designed to provide donations and expenses for your reports to the Elections Spending Commission. Filing can be a challenge, so I call the Commission for support, because penalties are stiff if there is a mistake.

CANDIDATE SUPPORT

The majority of Maui County Progressive candidates have gone through the Kuleana Academy's in-depth political leadership training. Based out of Kaui, those who graduate run for elected office, manage political campaigns or deepen their community organizing and engagement. The Kuleana Academy also provides legislative advocacy support and training at the County and State levels. Once their 12-weekend training is complete, need a local vehicle to provide ongoing support to the elections. Also, they need to understand the local landscape, issues and help with building name recognition. That is where the Maui Pono Network steps in.

We function as an extension of their individual campaign team. Non-incumbent Progressive Candidates receive ongoing coaching and feedback. Candidate encouragement is often required, as running for office can seem like a huge struggle.

The MPN team acts as a communicator amplifier. We are developing a network of support for all progressive candidates and ask for their input and collaboration. This teamwork occurs well before the elections and continues when elected.

Candidates you are supporting should be aware of and support all the platform issues. They should be well-versed in the history of the problem, impact on the community, position of opposing candidates, and proven solutions. They should understand how the county government functions.

In 2018, we had nine candidates who had not held office, and many did not have a good understanding of the issues. In response, we held a workshop for them.

Platform Workshop: We developed a workbook with the nine platform issues, their impacts, and possible solutions. Progressive County Council Members presented all the material to 23 participants, with another large group viewing over the Internet. It was lively, with many insightful questions and discussions. The workshop lasted 4 hours and also included discussing the inner workings of our County government.

Debates and Forums: Much of this training was preparation for the debates, which associations and organized groups sponsored throughout the island. Most were televised on Akaku, our local public access station. The newspapers would do write- ups and social media clips. I attended all 22 debates in 2018. Several of us would provide feedback and coaching after each session. This was an important stage for the Ohana Candidates, as residents were tuning into the debates; the candidates got needed exposure, and it did not cost them money.

In 2020, Zoom made these candidate exchanges much more accessible in a variety of formats. Our producer, Daniel Smith, who was able to edit opposing views in sequence for the same questions, made engaging 3-minute clips that were very telling.

Some of the candidates required additional coaching on presentation skills. We had several practice speaking on video and provided statistics to build arguments. Other counseling involved issues of self-esteem, confidence, and interpersonal communication improvements.

An important note. Observe candidate encounters with potential voters. Particularly notice the energy exchange. The most important exchange is not the words themselves, but the energy behind the words. Some candidates need help with developing Emotional Intelligence in front of groups. We shot video at all the events and used it as feedback for coaching.

EVENTS FOR GRASSROOTS AND CANDIDATES

Earth Day Event: This was the first big event for candidates in April 2018 and in 2020. The celebration and awareness event was produced by Bruce Douglas, a Steering Committee member. This was his twenty-fourth year of staging the event. The Maui Pono Network team worked as backstage support.

In 2018, it was a colorful gathering, with great food and vendors. The venue had a big stage, and many bands played throughout the day. Over 1,800 people attended! Candidates spoke about why they were running and what they would bring to that office. We also got to see how they presented themselves, and interviewed several, as we were in the process of finalizing our candidate selection.

In 2020, the virtual event drew 2,300 viewers on Facebook live and was also shown on local TV. All the Progressive candidates had a time slot in-between musicians and presenters. Even in the virtual world it was a success, as it provided early exposure for candidates.

Monthly Potluck: We held monthly potlucks in 2018. Each

event featured guest speakers who drew in a wide range of people. Walter Ritte Jr. was our first speaker; he was the leader who wanted to stop the Navy's use of Kahoolawe for bombardment training.

154

These meetings fueled people's involvement. Afterwards, we had Ohana Candidates speak. By filming them, we would have another coaching and promotion tool.

Virtual broadcasts are another way to have noted speakers and candidates address attendees. It was effective in 2020. This, however, does not compare to having a gathering with your community. Isolation is not our nature! Ideally have live streaming and video at all physical gathering events to expand outreach and participation.

Meet-and-Greets: Sponsored by citizens who invite their neighbors to meet candidates. Personal contact is the top priority in capturing votes. When candidates talk about their platform, vision and ways to change the system in an intimate setting, they win votes. The people who attend often ask great questions of the candidates and come away impressed. Many become donors or volunteers for the candidate. Some of our elected candidates felt that this was one of the most effective strategies in getting elected, as it became the main source of their campaign volunteers and donations.

STEP 5 LOCAL ELECTIONS

CAMPAIGN STRATEGIES

The Maui Pono Network's intention was to be an extension of the candidates' campaign team. Each candidate had his or her own campaign manager. Their core campaign group can be two or twenty volunteers. We developed a team approach. We would ask how we can support them and there were two requests that stood out. So, we offer sign/banner and video services to all our candidates. We also developed the most cost/effective grassroots campaign strategies.

Banners/Signs: In Maui, there is a tradition of plastering each intersection with campaign signs from May to November during an election year. The Ohana Candidates wanted a presence, so we were strategic. We repeated our brand and image by using the same layout as our handout cards, social media blasts, Web presence, and postal mailings.

We started by taking professional pictures of the candidates. Bruce Douglas oversees this and looks for the right expression from the eyes. Bruce also designs their banners and signs, and gets them printed and shipped at very low cost, in part because of the volume. Bruce even makes life-size signs of the candidates that are a big hit.

The MPN had supported a total of 670 banners and large signs for the primary and general elections. 150 were life-size cut-outs, as well as smaller signs. This also includes 200, 18 sq. ft, Ohana Candidates' banners set up throughout the county. Daniel Smith mapped out all the key legal areas to put up signs and banners and set up over 400 of them.

Video Production: We developed both 30-second and 2-minute video spots. We made oppositional spots and targeted messages that evoke emotions. Our producer, Daniel Smith made 42 videos in 2020 that included the coup, 7 charter amendments, interviews, candidate differences and candidate profiles. They were posted on our county television station, social media and our web site. The MPN web site alone had 128,198 visits through the 2020 elections.

'Ohana Candidate Cards: The Maui Pono Network designed, printed and distributed 20,000 'Ohana Candidate cards for the Primary and 20,000 for the 2020 general election. Distribution included our progressive network, door hangers, mailing, grocery stores, and distribution centers. The social media 'Ohana card reached 38,450 people on Facebook and was shared by 428 reaching 63% of county voters. To put these numbers in perspective, there were 92,000 registered Maui County voters in 2020 with 61,000 ballots received.

In 2018, we focused on personal contact at public community events. The Maui Pono Network handed out 88,000 'Ohana Candidate cards in our county, at 36 events, over a 6-month period. If an event does occur, we will have a team there to hand out cards. We also had distribution centers at local stores.

Memes: These effective communication tools influence the community narrative. The Maui Pono Network shared 282 posts and produced 58 original memes for the 2020 elections, with up to 30,000 views per month just on Facebook. Some stood out -- like the County Council Report Card, which reached 16,200, water rights -15,000, the Super PAC coup attempt -14,800. Also, the MPN had significant activity on Instagram.

Social Media: Some issues and memes generated a lot of discussion. Sylvia Litchfield monitored thousands of comments and questions starting back in March, to November. The feedback allowed us to continuously improve. It was valuable feedback to see how we were impacting the community narrative. Fuel the community dialogue about the candidates and issues by utilizing targeted posts with short videos and memes.

Letters to the Editor: A constant stream of pro 'Ohana "letters to the editor" was printed in three local papers. This was, in part, aided by our call to writers and providing a template and submission instructions on our website. It is the most-read section of the newspaper and reached a critical audience, senior citizens.

Sign-Waving: Another Maui tradition is sign-waving along

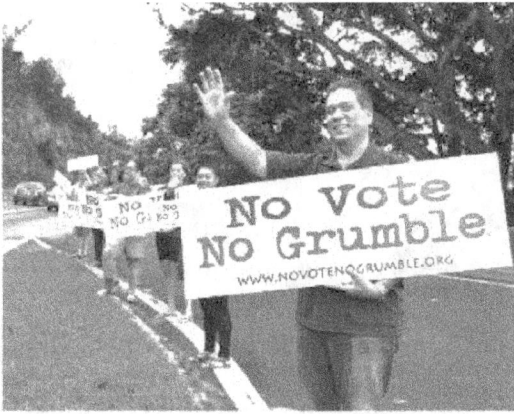

the side of the roads during rush hour. The good old boy network candidates would pay union workers to wave signs. They would have as many as 60 people in one big pack along the road. The Ohana Candidates got together with their volunteer supporters every Friday at a busy spot, waving signs and had a party atmosphere that made it fun. It has a limited impact for actual votes, but those who wave signs help with team-building as they express their enthusiasm and physically gather with others in 2020.

Phone Canvassing: The automated dialing system and call-tracking made this productive and engaging. One campaign team utilized the system the most, making nearly 12,000 calls. A total of 28 callers participated in October connecting with Maui County Voters. It is important to develop a phone list through purchase and networking with members. Prepare a script and train volunteers. It has become an even more important tool with the imposition of medical martial law.

Mailings: We mailed 21,000 cards for targeted district voting in 2020. We used the same design as the handout card for branding purposes. County voters should receive the card on the same day the mail-in ballots are received. For county-wide mailings, we relied on other progressive organizations to take that on because of the expense and limited impact. The big-money corporate opposition was sending up to 20 mailers in a month. We needed a cost-effective way to challenge that and rise above the fray. Our door-hangers were a great success.

Information Door-Hangers: The MPN printed, volunteers assembled, and deliverers distributed 16,000 information packets to the front doors of targeted areas in Maui County. The packet included cartoons on the 7 Charter Amendments, the candidate report card and candidate flyers. If we met someone willing to talk to us, that was a bonus.

Personal Canvassing: Personal relations are the most important vote-getter. Go door-to-door on targeted well-populated streets, if permissible. It was a big disadvantage to not be able to do that in districts where we wanted to remove the incumbent. We did interact at store entrances. Candidates did go regularly to the farmers' markets when they opened in 2020.

The use of this important strategy is obviously questionable with the unknowns of medical martial law. Do the rounds. If a candidate starts early in the day, he or she is able to go door-to-door on populated streets. It is important to target the demographics the candidate needs to connect with. Going door-to-door is also a good way to distribute lawn signs. It takes a commitment to connect in this way, and candidates can learn a lot from these informal conversations.

Education: Have handout material on platform issues, and the solutions your candidates stand for. Provide information on voting records and donors of candidates. Use the County Council rooms to testify about your platform issues. Your website should be an information hub, with links to all the candidates you support. Memes go a long way. Use facts and make your message clear.

The Ohana Candidates had a presence at all the community events and final debates. We did all we could think of, including a presence at all of the polling stations on Election Day. I used to run cross-country when I was in high school. That last half-mile was a grind. That last push to the finish line in the elections had parallels. But it was well worth the tremendous effort.

VICTORY IN 2018 AND 2020

Happy Pono Network supporters toast after the third printout results were announced Tuesday at Akaku Maui Community Media's election-night block party in Kahului. 'Ohana Coalition-backed candidates took five of nine Council seats and have gained a Progressive majority in the County Council.

The following is an article from the *Maui News* the day after the 2018 elections.[21] "A major victory for Maui Ohana candidates in Tuesday's election is likely to signal a sea change in direction for Maui's County Council. A majority of Ohana candidates were ushered into power in the Council.

The new activist blood includes Molokaʻi's Keani Rawlins-Fernandez, Shane Sinenci representing East Maui, Natalie "Tasha" Kama, who beat retiring Maui Mayor Alan Arakawa for the Kahului seat in a stunning upset, and Tamara Paltin in West Maui, with Kelly King retaining her South Maui seat by a huge majority.

"I'm humbled, honored, and excited, not just for me," says Keani Rawlins-Fernandez, who beat once-popular incumbent Stacey Crivello for the Molokaʻi seat. "We got the majority on the Council, which is amazing, and we almost have a supermajority of women (6 of 9members). Maui County is definitely leading the way."

"We're not going to be stalling anymore," she emphasizes. "We're going to get down to work, and we each bring a different skill set and experience. All of that will complement each other. We are all very action-oriented. We want to get things done, and that's why we ran in the first place. For me, one of my biggest frustrations in the last few years was how much stalling occurred, like with polystyrene containers. That bill could have been passed so much faster, but that was not what the (Council) majority wanted. They held it off as long as possible.

Feeling hopeful about the future of Maui, she concludes: "In 2014, when people came out and voted for the (GMO) moratorium and it wasn't upheld, it hurt a lot of people. It was such a betrayal of trust that many people refused to come out [and vote] in 2016. I feel hope was restored with this election."

Several days after the 2018 election, the Maui Pono Network put on a celebration of unity for all of the county's elected officials. We wanted to emphasize Pono and Aloha as we move forward with this new administration. Now it was no longer about opposition; it was a hope for a new dawn. One where the majority of the County Council are unified in their support for the land and people.

From the expression and intention in the moment, it felt that an important shift had occurred. There were people in the crowd crying with joy and relief, as a long-term goal had been realized: the unified representation focused on the people and environment. This was not an empty celebration, but a landmark moment.

Within a short time, entrenched department heads were voted out by the new County Council and replaced by bright, experienced, and creative coordinators. The $90 million-dollar construction project that primarily enriched GOBN was canceled. Funds were being allocated for affordable housing. They settled the long-standing injection well case. Made it so the community associations must approve development. They proposed seven Charter Amendments, which were passed in 2020, that would rewire the county system to serve the common good. It would increase transparency, end cronyism and increase citizens' participation.

Big money, out-of-county, corporate Super PACs responded with a vengeance in the 2020 county elections, spending $430,000 in the last 40 days of the election. They endorsed and promoted the exact opposite of the Maui Pono Network (MPN), including its Ohana Candidate slate. The Maui Pono Network help stopped this attempted coup of our local governance.

It was a David-and-Goliath story. Voters selected 14 of the 16 candidates and charter amendments the MPN supported. The MPN's budget was $10,000 for the general elections, $1/43^{rd}$ of the opposition's budget.

Now, six of the seven charter amendments are being enacted. Maui County governance will never be the same. This is the community reset we should aspire to. Do not fall into the illusion that you are not empowered. You are! We are all empowered to bring about systemic change!

It doesn't end after the elections. Our small group continues to focus on supporting this new system. It does take work and focus to maintain, but the relatively small effort can bring about uplifting change and an actual reset to home rule and the common good.

STEP 6 - BUILD LOCAL MOMENTUM FOR HOME RULE

REWIRING FOR COMMON GOOD SYSTEMS

This book has been about a rewiring of sorts. The rewiring is both internal and external. Internally it begins with the way our subconscious was unconsciously manipulated through social engineering, affecting our perception and behavior. Systems designed to subjugate the masses require covert means that involve manipulating beliefs.

Consciousness is the primary battlefront; it is what sustains the delusion, and also what can end it. False beliefs act as filters, affecting the capacity to listen to a deeper truth and to be aware of what is being done in the name of democracy. The rewiring involves removing false subconscious beliefs that disempower and delude.

As you take the rewiring externally, it requires connecting with others and being part of your community. This is the source of the resurgence, creating a force for change with others. The power lies in the collective.

Common Good systems are wired to spread local empowerment to the many. There is openness and collaboration. It can be a one-time event or a long-term commitment to a cause. It generates a greater ownership and participation in local community development. A wide variety of organizational strategies illustrated in this text can be used to engage participation.

The distinctive wiring characteristic of the Elite system is its consolidation, centralization and control of power into the hands of the few. Rewiring government and corporate control involves moving away from consolidation and hierarchy. It means having resources more locally controlled with transparency. This local empowerment involves the elected seats of counties, cities, and local towns.

The majority of the Council or Board have the power to allocate funds, allow permits, support local action. They can use that power to develop the commons or address important needs like food security. For example, the Maui County Agriculture Department that was formed with the passing of the 2020 charter amendments. It provides small and medium-size farmers the needed support to address the islands' 90% dependency on imported food. The County Department of Agriculture promotes food sustainability and resiliency and boosts economic growth in the agricultural sector. It's a boon to our community to have access to healthy organic food. Also, the water plan and development moved to this department, overseen by an Ohana Council member. Now the community can address the corporate control of our water and bring it into the public domain. This is what happens with Home Rule.

Realize there is local control over income generated in their domain. In some counties, it exceeds property taxes. They can rewire the allocation of tax revenue to *not* support corruptions. Imagine trillions of dollars supporting our communities and environment instead of war, pollution, citizen surveillance and subjugation.

167

THE CHALLENGE OF CANDIDATE BETRAYAL

There have been many instances where candidates are elected through a significant grassroots effort, only to become a different person of a different moral character. Regardless whether the intention was to dupe his or her supporters, or if the acquisition of power awakened some latent part of themselves, the results are the same.

Maui Pono Networks' first outing in 2018 had over 200 volunteers campaigning vigorously for Tasha Kama's election against the seated Mayor of Maui County. I personally spent considerable time coaching and mentoring her, and was also her constant cheerleader. She won by a landslide.

The first important vote by the new County Council was on the County Directors' positions. The existing Corporate Council Head was a big reason the good old boy network had such a stranglehold on the County. That very first vote for this new County Council was a crucial one regarding who really controls the county.

I was in the County Chambers when Tasha cast her vote to keep him in office. There were gasps and outcries from the audience that were silenced by the banging of the gavel. Her vote hit me in my heart; I felt it sink to the point where I became nauseous. I wanted to vomit and scream at the same time. As soon as the meeting was adjourned, I went up to Tasha and said, "What is happening? You have just torn my heart open! What happened to the values and commitment you gave to all your supporters?" I was deeply upset and she suggested we meet.

When I sat in her office the following day, she offered some strange rationale for her vote, based on her meeting with the Corporate Council Head. When I left her office, I noticed it was sandwiched between the two women on the Council who always support the wishes of the good old boy network. Tasha's secretary was Mike White's former assistant. Mike, the former Council Chair, was notorious for his big-money connections. While leaving, I even got a smirk from one of those Council members sitting next to Tasha as I met her stare. It was a look that said, "I got you!"

We got screwed by a grandmother in her 70s! She would not see me or any Progressives who vigorously supported her, from that point on. Her discussions were focused on corporate lobbyists. Her voting record says it all. She voted with one of her compatriots who shared the same wall. On every single key vote, she went against the Ohana Candidates' vote.

Do not be deflated if one of the candidates you support decides to go the big money route. This story has been repeated throughout our election history. One Mayor who was elected through grassroots efforts had wild sexual affairs and openly displayed drug use once he was in power. Some got bribed as the skeletons in their closet still lingered. Some worshipped money and power and were offered a king's ransom. It is part of the democratic process to have an opportunity to remove these people from office, even if there is a wait to the next election.

There is a bright side to this, however. There was one centrist on the County Council. He finally came around to support Progressive causes. The Progressive majority was retained.

HAVE PROGRESSIVE LIAISONS

The common good system requires constant vigilance and development. Once the Progressives are in office, there needs to be a system to help assure that worthy Progressives remain in office. This requires monitoring county decisions and giving specific feedback if someone doesn't keep their promise. The Elite corporate System will create pressure from propaganda and manipulation. Big money will try to take control back from the people. What happened in Maui County's 2020 coup attempt is a good example. Monitoring is crucial, so that backdoor deals and policies are not forced on unsuspecting people.

There is a bond of trust and respect through working closely with the candidate during the campaign. It is a symbiotic relationship that involves community development for the Common Good and supporting candidates who align with these goals. If those you have elected are not following through with their promises, they must be held responsible.

This illustrated the importance and need to have ongoing Progressive Liaison. The Maui Pono Network provides such a staff to Interface between County Council Members on important issues, communicate among Progressive organizations and inform the Maui County public. Aja Eyre is Maui Pono Network's representative.

A liaison can propose cost-effective solutions to community needs and increase awareness of repercussions from decisions. Sunshine Law prevents elected officials from having discussions outside of Chambers and can be a communication bridge. Also, the liaison serves as a communication amplifier on important county meetings, votes and issues. Keeping the community narrative alive between elections continues to build local momentum.

Developing a community into a democracy is an ongoing task.

CHARTER AMENDMENTS

The charter establishes the organizational structure of the county's legislative and executive branches, how the county is governed, how legislation is adopted, financial and ethics procedures, and how to amend the charter. These amendments provide support and a framework for Local Sustainability, Transparency, Business Development, Local Currency, Development of the Commons, and Election Integrity.

It is a living document. When conditions warrant change and the voters agree, the charter is amended to reflect those changes.

It has been that way since the first charter was adopted by Maui County voters in 1967. Much remains from that first charter in our current charter, which was adopted in 1982 and amended in almost every election cycle between 1984 and 2018.

The charter requires a mandatory review every 10 years by an 11-member Charter Commission. Maui County is due for another review starting in 2021. Prior to the 2020 election. all 11 appointments were made by the Mayor and resulted in legislation benefiting the corporate elite. With the newly passed charter amendment, he can select 2 to be on the charter commission; 9 are selected by each member of the County Council. This plugged a big portal for Corporate Rule. I was asked to be one of the 11 on the Charter Commission. It is an example of systemic change that happens when Home Rule is gained.

Charter amendments can be started by Council resolution or by petition to the Council or the county clerk. Council-initiated amendments require two readings and a super-majority vote by six Council members to place the matter on the election ballot. Here are six Charter Amendments passed for Maui County in 2020. This is an important part of systemic change on a local level.

- Extend and increase the affordable housing fund.

- Establish stricter term limits for council members by limiting the number of terms a person may serve to five two-year terms.

- Establish standards for interpreting and complying with the charter, including requiring judicial action to be filed within 30 days to seek clarity when a conflict in the interpretation of the charter is raised.

- Authorize the Council to appoint nine members and the mayor to appoint two members of the 11-member Charter Commission.

- Establish stricter term limits for the Mayor by limiting the number of terms a person may serve as Mayor to two full four-year terms.

- Establish a Department of Agriculture.

For many communities, these changes need to address the development of common public spaces for local exchanges like farmers' markets and swap meets. Pass local legislation to encourage the use of local currency and reduce dependence on the fiat Federal Reserve note. Bring your local utilities under public control.

Local support during this reset is vital if we want to avoid the New World Order that awaits. This all relies on the trigger for systemic change, as it takes the alignment of the majority of your Council and board. Out of that, the Common Good can thrive.

The ultimate end of all revolutionary social change is to establish the sanctity of human life, the dignity of man, the right of every human being to liberty and well-being. — Emma Goldman

CHAPTER 6

THE PRIMARY BATTLE ....BELIEFS

"Who looks outside, dreams; who looks inside, awakes." -- *Carl Jung*

The movie "Wizard of Oz" depicts an important lesson. Toto drew back the curtain to reveal the Wizard pulling an array of levers that put on a display to deceive the population. This tale gives a key strategy. Once the man behind the curtain was revealed, the wizard's mythical powers vanished and the travelers got all of their wishes fulfilled, finally realizing that the answer was always there ... inside them.

The wizards I am referring to are far more sinister than the Wizard of Oz. They are hidden by the curtain of the media, layers of bureaucratic maze, and "front people." They manipulate the levers that produce images to deceive and distract us from important topics affecting our lives.

This curtain of delusion is presently thick and opaque. The vast majority of the population go on with their daily routines not questioning what they are told, and yet an intuitive unease is telling many, "Something is deeply wrong." Instead of following this inner warning, they push on, earning money for mounting bills, watching mindless TV shows, or receiving irrelevant and partial propaganda disguised as news. However, the impact of the wizard's levers can be seen and strongly felt in the medical martial law, the destruction of businesses, depressed housing market, rising health care costs, devaluation of the dollar, the collusion of big business with government, escalating debt and runaway military spending. People are awakening to the levers and wiring of the corrupt Corporate Elite System.

Once the true nature of the Wizard of Oz is exposed, his mythical power disappears. We are now pulling back the curtain and exposing the 1% of the population who are controlling the levers that are choking this nation and planet.

We need to awaken to a revolution! Not a revolution based on anger, anarchy and pitchforks, but rather an evolution of awakening and empowering, starting from within. It's an evolution to empower individuals, communities, and counties to reclaim their sovereignty and fight for the democracy of their sovereigns: We the People.

176

THE MAIN CHALLENGE TO COMMUNICATION AND ORGANIZING

The primary challenge, the primary battle we face in making system change is within each of us. The skirmishes, which are to gain control of your subconscious beliefs, can shape perceptions that can lull society into fabricated illusion. Beliefs can help humanity either reach its highest potential, or its own enslavement.

Beliefs can be planted in us without our knowledge or consent. These distorted beliefs act as filters that narrow and delude our perception. They can be shaped by social engineering that involves a wide range of media, particularly television. We can be led to believe anything, including the false perception that we are powerless to change these corrupt systems.

Awakening is an internal process that shines a light on darkness that was set in our subconscious by ignorance and manipulation. Breaking through begins with an internal process that confronts belief systems about topics such as government, money, and well-being.

Explore the battlefront and the profound impact of subconscious beliefs in shaping our perception. They can shut down a global society. They can manipulate U.S. taxpayers to support imperialist wars in Afghanistan, Iraq, Sudan, Libya, and Yemen. Removing false beliefs allows awareness of the tyranny being committed so that we can end it. Understanding the formation mechanisms of these beliefs can help us remove them from the subconscious. We are more able to facilitate our own awakenings.

CONSCIOUNESS LAYERS

Underneath all we think is all we believe. Our beliefs shape our thoughts, direct our actions, and form our perception of the world we live in.

By far the most opaque blinders we have to the truth, the biggest block to accessing our true potential, lies within each of us. The structure of our conscious illustrates the most fundamental step we need to take in order to awaken to lasting, uplifting change. Ancient mystics knew that underneath our actions are the beliefs that, in some way, direct our thoughts and perceptions. According to modern-day psychologists like Carl Jung, this unconscious layer shapes over 90% of what we perceive, and forms a collective standpoint for creating our awareness of our world.

The unconscious false beliefs act as a barrier to the super-consciousness, our Higher Self. It is like looking down into a lake. If the surface has turbulence, like an unfocused awareness, you cannot see very deeply. If the water column is murky, like a subconscious filled with false beliefs, you will not be able to see to the depths, where the super-consciousness lies.

Layers of Consciousness

Awareness

Conscious Awareness is what we see and are aware of in the moment.

Non-Conscious Awareness processes our feelings and the bodily functions that come into conscious awareness when we focus on them (e.g., the sensations in your right toe).

Pre-Conscious Awareness is when we want to access knowledge, memories, language or information.

Unconscious

Unconscious Personal Beliefs are accumulated in many ways, including manipulation and distortion, to make you believe what is true or not true.

Collective Unconscious Beliefs come from our family, friends, community, and even nations, and are influenced by collective agreements that can be manipulated. Cultural conditioning is part of all this.

Super Conscious

Sub-Super Conscious involves a connection outside of our confined awareness, where intuition and insights awaken.

Super Conscious Mind is a high-vibration connection with Universal Consciousness.

That is why personal growth often involves the letting go of low-vibration beliefs like self-doubt, or blaming others for your circumstances. It is the peeling away of false perceptions that block a deeper awakening. I welcome bringing these dysfunctional false beliefs within me to my awareness, so I can let them go and have a less-obstructed connection to a higher consciousness. Understanding the influence, formation, and elimination of beliefs provides a key to ongoing awakenings. Question your beliefs. Remember, they are not fixed. You put them there, or unconsciously allowed them there; you can also remove them.

Since changing our beliefs about the existing exploitative system is an important step toward changing our societal systems, allow yourself to question your beliefs about our government, legal systems, voting system, Medical Martial Law, and vaccines.

BELIEFS

A belief is a deeply-rooted complex that has been established with conviction. Our beliefs shape not only what we do, but also how we see. They color how we perceive the world, and guide our thoughts, actions, and emotions, whether we are aware of them or not.

Our beliefs, which operate powerfully in our lives, affect our biochemistry, perceptions, digestion, glands, immune systems, and all aspects of our being. They have the power to make us sick or healthy. We cannot help but act according to our beliefs and live them out as our conceptual centers.

180

Our subconscious offers fertile ground in which to form an array of beliefs. As we take in our day-to-day experiences, we are bombarded by outside messages specifically designed to impact and shape our beliefs. Unconscious beliefs can be developed by those who control the media, or religious, government and monetary systems. When we hold a false belief, it can have harmful consequences.

These outside influences can program beliefs and create a new "reality" based on distortion and lies. In this way, a dream world has been woven by the Elite, fashioned around unsustainable material consumerism, divisiveness, fear, and dreams.

As a society, we need to awaken to the manipulation that has been herding us down a road of subjugation. The Elite's dream world reinforces fear, debt, separation, anger and violence.

If you believe that you must get the vaccine to be healthy, or these pandemic measures are justified, or the storm trooper police of the Elite will come and take you away, you drain your energy with fear, and probably delusion. Beliefs that diminish your energy are energy-drainers.

Have an uplifting vision, and take strategic action to make the vision happen. Encourage beliefs that cast a bright light onto your future, where darkness cannot exist. For our well-being, our beliefs should be energy-enhancing, not energy-draining.

Other beliefs, like those from Gandhi, focused on the power of love and forgiveness. He would teach others to develop local self-sufficiency while peacefully unplugging from corrupt systems. The belief in love and in helping our fellow humans is uplifting and energizing. There are many beliefs that uplift and support us, like a healthy self-esteem, or the vision of accomplishing a community project.

If the formation of beliefs can fuel the "War on Terror," why not use them for noble purposes? If beliefs are part of our make-up and how we function in the world, why not use them constructively? A belief in the power of love can change a person and a society for the good. We can use the power of beliefs to fuel initiatives for a peaceful transition from exploitive to common good systems.

The real battlefront involves false beliefs that deceive us and prevent us from seeing a deeper truth. The analogy of battle is appropriate, as these opposing forces invade the subconscious to deceive us into giving our wealth and well-being to a few self-proclaimed leaders. This invasion allows a sinister agenda to unfold. From the manipulation of the subconscious, we have become partially enslaved in the Elites' dream world, although most of us don't know it.

Our subconscious can be crafted to take actions that harm us, our family, and nation. We can even be lulled into a cultural trance. It all starts with the formation of beliefs.

182

THE FORMATION OF BELIEFS

Most people's subconscious forms and reinforces beliefs on a daily basis. We are flooded with undigested input, many times reinforcing a crafted message that settles into our mind. This input creates clusters or complexes of images and emotions that can form beliefs. Beliefs can be what is behind reactions, behaviors, and perceptions that continue, with little conscious awareness. In this way, we become influenced without really realizing it.

The majority of citizens in Nazi Germany were led to believe the deception of their glorious future until the deck of cards fell. The 1% pulling the strings knows the subtle tools of propaganda that were used then, and have developed them since. Because the ruling elite control the media, they can spin whatever information they want to make the impressions they want. To implant false beliefs, you simply model the process based on the belief's natural formation.

Belief Formation

1. A major event occurs, or there is a constant reinforcement of a message.

2. We interpret the event and make a decision: This is what I need to do to succeed, or to take care of my health, or to make sense of it.

3. We have a feeling of certainty about that decision.

4. We look for, and find, further proof that we have made a good decision. We ignore or deny evidence to the contrary.

5. Our belief begins to dictate the world we co-create and experience.

CONFRONTING BELIEF SYSTEMS

At age twenty-eight, I was owner and president of a growing environmental consulting company in Anchorage, Alaska, that had nine employees. However, success just seemed to cause me more stress. I often worked late into the night by myself. Even though I had seasoned professionals on-staff, I was carrying all the weight of the business. Finally, I could no longer ignore the fact that I simply wasn't delegating enough. I had a pattern of mistrust, a habit of not including others in my decisions. This pattern interfered with openness, and with teamwork.

As I reflected on the pattern, I saw that it had taken root during my teenage years. Back then, the impact of the belief was slight and negligible. Like a stick thrown into a slow stream, it barely caused a ripple. But as the stream picked up speed—as my business and employees all amplified my pattern—the stick began causing larger and larger eddies. The pattern became apparent.

When I was fourteen, I had a lawn-mowing business. I took care of twelve lawns in the neighborhood. Once, I hired a kid to help me while I went away to camp. Unfortunately, he did a bad job. I had just returned home from cleaning up the kid's mess and apologizing to my clients when I ran into my dad, whom I loved and respected. He consoled me, with his hand on my shoulder, here's what he said: "If you want something done right, do it yourself."

His comment became my conviction. It buried itself in my subconscious mind, and took root as a belief. Now, for the first time, I could see it clearly.

Awareness of the belief, along with my realization that the belief no longer served me, was the first step toward uprooting it. Then I took active measures. When I gathered my staff in the conference room and asked for their help in eliminating this dysfunctional pattern, they actually stood up and cheered. I got plenty of support from my staff. I developed delegation skills, encouraged entrepreneurship, and expanded my trust. I let go of the conviction that I had to do everything myself. Within a month, the negative pattern was essentially gone.

Once we integrate a belief, it becomes an unquestioned command to our nervous systems, dictates our actions and shapes our perceptions. It filters the energy we put out, and interprets the energy we take in. We unconsciously validate the ideas that spring from the belief, which generates a fixed pattern of behavior. In this way, beliefs blind us. *Over time, we actually become our beliefs,* as they become our frameworks for thinking, feeling, functioning, and relating. They shape our intentions and create our "sense of reality."

INTERPRETATIONS OF EVENTS SHAPE BELIEFS

Our belief systems are often acquired falsely. Repeated messages from the government, corporations, and media generate a perception that may be meant to hide the full truth. We hang onto misinterpretations and misconceptions about systems, others, and life itself.

For ten years, I led workshops that explored the way personal beliefs shape relationships. In one workshop, a woman said that her primary belief about relationships was, *"You can't trust men—they are out to get you."* At age 32, she had no relationships with men and yet wanted a male companion.

With some coaching, she uncovered the root experience of that belief. One day when she was 12 years old, she was visiting her cousin in her uncle's bar, and got cornered in the back room by one of the regular patrons. He grabbed her and planted a wet kiss on her mouth. She pushed him away, disgusted, walked out, and never told anyone. But she made a decision that men are disgusting and formed a belief that shaped her actions thereafter.

In this very same program, there was a man who touched me deeply by his loving interactions within our group of sixty participants. He exuded love. I could feel it coming right from his heart.

During one of the breaks, I asked this man what he had done to be in this loving energy space. He looked at me with a smile and

186

showed me his forearm, where there were numbers tattooed. He told me, "*During World War II, my parents, sister, two brothers, and I were all taken to Auschwitz. I was the only one to survive. While regaining my strength after I was freed, I had time to reflect on this experience. At times I felt anger and the discord of hate. But I saw how this negativity was impacting my recovery.*

"*Then I drew on another experience, reflecting on the love my family shared before being imprisoned. When I would envision my family, I would recall love and openness, and a surge of energy would enter my heart. I made a decision to hold that expansive energy in my heart versus the contracted energy of hate. I would live what my family taught me, not the hate of the prison camp. And that has been the belief I live on a daily basis.*"

One person suffered a forced kiss and chose to shut down her heart. Another suffered atrocities and chose to keep his heart open. It's not the events that create our beliefs. It's our decision about how we interpret the events that makes all the difference.

We can interpret the events created by the parasitic elite in a way that shuts down our heart and dampens our spirits. Or, we can be like the former Auschwitz prisoner who used his experiences as a way to focus on the power of love.

MANIPULATING MEMORY AND VIEWPOINTS

Memory is a sequence of rearranged data that shifts every time it is retrieved. Memory pieces together similar experiences, desires, justifications, and imaginations in the reconstruction mix. So, the reconstruction is never like the actual experience, and in fact becomes further distorted every time it is recalled.

Proteins are the building blocks of memory. If you block proteins from forming, you block memory. Likewise, when you recall, you also use proteins. Every time we access a memory, it is reconstructed with proteins. Every memory is built anew when accessed. Protein inhibitors can block memory formation and recall.

You can also create new memories after the incident. Memory is malleable. Media can be used to shape these memories for a purpose. Every time you recall, you reconstruct the memory with slight changes. Keep on adding false information in the aided recall, and you get a reconstruction that outside architects want. Our media and TV are a particularly important part of reconstructing memory to fit the Elite's purpose.

We can distort memories of previously experienced events, and can be easily coached to recall things that are not there, or hide things that are there. With this level of access to our subconscious beliefs, we can have our awareness filters altered by the media.

Elizabeth F. Loftus, an expert in memory recall, notes several cases that exposed this human back door. In 1986, Nadean Cool, a nurse's aide in Wisconsin, sought therapy from a psychiatrist to help her cope with her reaction to a traumatic event experienced by her daughter. During therapy, the psychiatrist used hypnosis and other suggestive techniques to dig out buried memories of abuse that Cool herself had allegedly experienced. In the process, Cool became convinced that she had repressed memories of having been in a satanic cult, of eating babies, of being raped, of having sex with animals, and of being forced to watch the murder of her eight-year-old friend. Cool came to believe that she had more than 120 personalities, children, adults, angels and even a duck, all because she was told she had experienced severe childhood sexual and physical abuse. The psychiatrist also performed exorcisms on her, one of which lasted for five hours, and included the sprinkling of holy water, and the use of a cross with screams to Satan to leave Cool's body.

When Cool finally realized that false memories had been planted, she sued the psychiatrist for malpractice. In March 1997, after five weeks of a trial, her case was settled out of court for $2.4 million. And Nadean Cool is not the only patient to develop false memories as a result of implanted memories.

In Missouri in 1992, a church counselor helped Beth Rutherford to remember during therapy that her father, a clergyman, had regularly raped her between the ages of 7and 14, and that her mother sometimes helped him by holding her down. Under her therapist's guidance, Rutherford developed memories of her father twice impregnating her and forcing her to abort the fetus herself with a coat hanger. The father had to resign from his post as a clergyman when the allegations were made public. Later medical examination of the daughter revealed, however, that she was still a virgin at age 22, and had never been pregnant. The daughter sued the therapist and received a $1-million settlement in 1996.

Loftus's research into memory distortion goes back to the early 1970s, when she began studies of the "misinformation effect." These studies show that when people who witness an event are later exposed to new and misleading information about it, their recollections often become distorted. In one example, participants viewed a simulated automobile accident at an intersection with a stop sign. After the viewing, half the participants received a suggestion that the traffic sign was a yield sign. When asked later what traffic sign they remembered seeing at the intersection, those who had been given the suggestion tended to claim that they had seen a yield sign. Most of those who had not received the phony information were more accurate in their recollection that the traffic sign was a stop sign.

Misinformation has the potential for invading our memories. After more than two decades of exploring the power of misinformation, researchers have learned a great deal about the conditions that make people susceptible to memory modification. Memories are more easily modified, for instance, when the passage of time allows the original memory to fade. Now many videos and articles that expose Corporate Rule and the facts on the pandemic are being erased from the memory of the Internet.

False messages are being constantly woven to create images and construction of a fake reality. For example, the CIA's involvement in developing Al Qaeda, ISIS and the drug trade is well-documented; and it is their made-up chaos that justifies their existence. See CorbettReport.com on topics related to Al Qaeda, ISIS.

Therapists could stir up such opposition from their patients to their parents when their reasoning is totally made-up. We are dealing with a barrage of distortions that create a false cultural trance that can easily pit neighbor against neighbor, and nation against nation.

CULTURAL TRANCE

The distortion and reshaping of memories, and the fabrication of misleading beliefs are the major weapons of the elite few to keep the masses in line with their deception. The veil of delusion is thick.

Look under the veil. Consider the global crisis in 2020. There is a virus that has caused deaths, but why are hospitals claiming death by Covid-19 when people were dying of cancer or heart failure? Why have there been unprecedented measures to shut down, isolate and sequester communities. Why are there so many measures to erode our freedom over something most people don't even know they have, because the symptoms are mild at this stage? Is there a need to inject the planet with an experimental biological agent? Is that a reason to restructure society so the 99% lose their liberties and large corporations rule the roost?

But the messages that don't address these questions go on like a mantra, feeding fear into all activities. The bio security state and its laws took flight in 2001 with the anthrax attacks. It was later shown that the origin was the U.S. military, although it was blamed on a lonely scientist who conveniently committed suicide just before he was apprehended. Then there was the constant barrage of movies showing global destruction because of some nasty contagion, usually turning people into flesh-eating zombies.

Familiarity plants the messages in our subconscious. The routine of thoughts and behavior creates a trance. So, we go on automatic pilot. It's like the frog that is placed in a pot of water without a lid. Gradually, the pot is heated to a boil. If the pot is heated slowly enough, the frog will remain in the pot, even though it could easily leap to safety. However, because it is unconscious of the slowly changing conditions, it stays in the pot and allows itself to be cooked.

In the same way, we are sometimes immersed in dysfunctional patterns that slowly kill off our potential. In our trance, we forget that we can actually change our environment. We stay put, as the dysfunction boils away our creativity, our potential, and our spirit. When a group allows itself to be boiled away, to adapt to dysfunction, that is what underlies cultural trance. We could easily jump out of that pot if we chose to.

In a physical trance, we lose voluntary movement and our actions become unconscious. In a cultural trance, we accept and perpetuate the environment, without question. George Ivanovich Gurdjieff, the Russian philosopher, called this cultural trance a *"false personality."*

We are shaped and reshaped by our cultural context. We actually construct many habits of our thinking and perceptions to reflect the consensus of what our cultures deem important. Ordinary awareness aligns itself to fit the culture. We start to assume that our cultural context is, in fact, reality.

The most prevalent causes of cultural trance are trust, complacency and leadership's suppression of change. A cultural trance is reinforced by a defeatist acceptance of "fate," particularly when people believe they do not have the power to change. People often feel and understand their trance, but are fearful to speak up. As time passes, the dysfunctional pattern fades into the background, filtered from their conscious awareness. In the end, what may *not* be normal becomes the norm.

What are some of the reinforced beliefs that paralyze much of the population from being involved with demanding change? Here is a partial list of the many untrue beliefs in the U.S. that discourage us from making change.

Untrue Beliefs Preventing System Change

- The United States stands for democracy and freedom, and its leaders are guided by what serves its citizens. So there is no need for concern.

- We must sacrifice our freedoms and rights to fight this global Pandemic or War on Terror, and must comply with what the government wants "for the good of all."

- We are dependent on the Federal and State governments for our safety and well-being.

- The 99% is disempowered to make changes on a grassroots level.

- The Elite's systems are too vast, confusing, and compartmentalized to understand, let alone change.

- The Federal Reserve and the business of printing money are owned by the Federal Government.

- Since the information we get from TV and the print media is fair and balanced, there is no need to question what we are told.

TRANSFORMING BELIEFS

Personal growth involves confronting and transforming self-limiting or destructive beliefs. Our societal growth requires a similar introspection. Our growth as a community and a nation requires removing the distortions implanted in our collective subconscious. If you put them there or were receptive to them, you can remove them. Below are insights into the formation of these beliefs and effective methods for changing them.

Transforming Belief Transformation Process

1. Question the premise of the belief: How did it form, what decisions did you make? You may have been led astray. You may have made a decision about an event that happened when you were five years old. You may believe the government's propaganda. Dysfunctional beliefs are founded on false premises. Question the premise and conclusion, go to the actual facts.

2. Realize the repercussions of the dysfunctional belief. What have been the consequences, what are you getting? The quickest way to change a belief is to associate it with pain and suffering.

3. Focus on joy and love, and the low-vibration beliefs will drop away, as they are not being fed the energy that sustains them.

4. Create an "empowered belief": Align a new belief with the greater truth of who you are and what you would like your community to become. An empowered belief is an affirmation and is the antithesis of the dysfunctional belief. The empowered belief should be:
   - expressed in the present tense
   - stated positively about changing yourself, or creating a vision
   - said in a way that evokes deep feeling and passion within you
   Example: *"I, Paul, am joyously supporting systemic change."*

5. Get support for your empowered belief and utilize this reinforcement, which can come from family, friends, business associates, a grassroots group, or a higher power.

195

Tools for Change

- Start with a different belief that supports what you want.

- Reinforce your new belief by getting others involved to support it.

- Pain is the ultimate tool for shifting an old belief. Look at the facts and the pain and suffering that occurs by staying with the old way. Look at what Corporate Rule brings.

- Model from other successes. The template is laid out in the book.

- Use positive affirmations to attract what you want.

Replace the beliefs that keep you participating in a system that fuels evil. When you believe, you can resolve community needs locally. When you believe, you can be joyous and partake in the abundance that surrounds us. When you believe, there is hope. When you believe you can, you can.

Focus on the belief that we can get out of this societal mess. We can release ourselves from corporate rule and the bleak world it offers. We can remove the shackles of this sociopathic system. There is a clear path blazed in Chapter 5. Affirm that it has manifested.

LAW OF ATTRACTION

Each of us can play a role in the shift to Home Rule by the thoughts and energy we hold. To see how this works we need to dive into our essence. Everything is made from a primordial quantum energy field. The energy we are made of is connected to another dimension. Science has shown that this energy moves between dimensions. We are inherently connected to something much bigger than our physical universe. The manifestation of our universe is dependent upon the underlying implicate order.[22] This connection is ongoing, even though it may not be on the radar screen of our awareness. Through this connection, we can access unbounded potential. But the rules are different because you are operating in the implicate order, this connected subtle dimension involves thoughts, and emotion.

Consciousness shapes the potential energy that makes our physical existence. Six thousand years ago, Bronze Age sages were contemplating the transition of the all-pervasive potential energy into physical form. For these Sankhya mystics, it isn't only energy that exists beyond our physical dimension. There is also consciousness. It is independent of energy, but merges with it in this physical realm. When consciousness merges with potential energy, it creates an information field.

Scientists in the field of quantum mechanics have discovered that the moment they inquire into the nature of subatomic particles, what they are looking for happens. If they want to find an electron

197

with no spin, they find it. If they think about an electron with no velocity or no momentum, then the electron they study will acquire those characteristics. [23]

THE INFORMATION FIELD

The laws of this subtle dimension follow the implicate order where the field is non-linear and responds instantaneously, regardless of distance, and attracts similar frequencies and manifestations. Like attracts like. Our thoughts and feelings are being broadcast.

These vibrations extend out from us. This subtle energy travels unobstructed through things we consider physically impenetrable; after all, it's all energy. Our information fields are extending out, attracting our reality.

We are literally a broadcast tower sending out energy vibrating at a certain frequency. This vibratory energy we send out attracts a similar energy vibration. It seeks a vibration match. We actually beam out and attract what we are feeling and thinking about most of the time.

Whatever energy we extend is the energy we attract. Like attracts like, in this subtle energy realm, and it functions in the implicate order.

Each and every component that makes up our life experience is drawn to us by the powerful Law of Attraction's response to the thoughts we think, and our feelings. This societal reset, our financial assets, our body's wellness, how we are treated, work satisfaction, and rewards—the very happiness of our life experience in general—is all happening because of the story that we tell and the beliefs that we hold.

To a certain extent, the story that we are led to believe, that we then repeat as true, helps attracts that reality. If we follow fear-generated news, watch movies and shows that evoke fear and violence and dwell on it, we will attract a vibrational match. If we chose to believe in and focus on joy and new ways of framing our societal structure, we will help attract that.

When we acknowledge our power, and then ask ourselves, "*What is it that I do want?*" we begin a gradual shift into the telling of our new story and into a much-improved point of attraction. The realization that something is not as we want it to be is an important first step. However, once we have identified that, the faster we are able to turn our attention in the direction of a solution, the better.

The problem is at a different vibration frequency than the solution. It is a different consciousness, and that shift happens when you see the vision of change, and believe you can make it happen, instead of dwelling on the problem. Focus on what you want, versus what you don't want.

A great way to check what you are thinking is to check what you are feeling. If you are happy, you are focusing on what you want.

If you are annoyed or angry, you are often focusing on what you don't want.

The Law of Attraction is responding to our vibration frequencies, and we can change our frequency of attraction. It can start simply by being happy and having a positive attitude. We attract what we feel and think about most of the time.

When it is asked with heartfelt feelings, it is given. We think we are asking with words, or even with action, and sometimes we are, but the Universe is not responding to our words or our action. The Universe is responding to our vibration, our information field made of our emotions and consciousness.

ATTRACTING A VIBRATION MATCH

The spectrum of color is associated with specific frequencies and vibrations. At the lower vibration, it is red. At the highest vibration, the light is white. In a similar way, our energetics can vibrate at a higher level -- into the white light. By energetic, I am referring to a measurable, experiential energy vibration always present within us, whether we are conscious of it or not.

Our energy vibrates at different levels, like the electromagnetic spectrum. We are always vibrating. Moods and emotions are our feeling sense of it. When our energy is vibrating at a high level, we feel uplifted, loved, and expansive. Our vibration more closely aligns with the high-vibrating quantum energy in the subtle dimension. In that emotional state of unconditional love, we become more of a vibrational match with the threshold of our physical universe.

That is why Jesus emphasized love so often in his teachings. *'Love the Lord your God with all your heart and with all your soul and with all your mind.' 'Love your neighbor as yourself.'*

Love is a vibration that is concentrated in our heart, which permeates our entire energy field. That vibration is a key to unlock a door to a higher dimension. Just as in the implicate order energy is in a relational field, we become consciously aware of the oneness we share when our emotions reside in the love frequency.

Our thoughts hold power. Why not use that power wisely, in a way that helps co-create Common Good Systems? Awaken to your power. Affirm uplifting beliefs about yourself and your community.

A CONSCIOUSNESS SHIFT

When we see through distorted collective unconscious and personal beliefs, several facts come more clearly into view, especially if you are familiar with the Appendix. First, we are not bound to support systems that exploit the masses by being based on deception. Thomas Jefferson encouraged radical house-cleaning of government in order to remove corruption. This is feasible through a decentralized, but connected, grassroots effort. Here a few points to support a belief and information fields that can peacefully change the system.

Affirming System Change

- The systems created by the Elite only function because the 99% participate. Refuse to utilize or support Elite Corporate Systems, cut off the flow of energy and it will wither.

- A growing number of citizens are pulling back this veil of delusion and realizing that wealth disparities and hardships stem from constitutional violations that the citizens actually have the power to remedy.

- Awakening from this delusion can be as easy as turning on a light switch; it is a dark fear that disappears in the light of truth and experience.

- We are sovereign Beings; the only one above us is the Creator. The *"Laws of Nature and of Nature's God"* entitle us to our Liberty. No man or government rules over us against our will;

we are free. This is the foundation of America, which is founded on the principles in the Declaration of Independence.

- New localized systems of service and exchange can develop rapidly through collaboration around community needs. They are free from control by the Corporate Elite System. Home Rule can facilitate local Charter Amendments to support this goal.

- The community, through collaboration, has the power and resources to develop new initiatives, without significant fiat currency and the use of local exchange.

- Through grassroots organizing of the 99%, we can become a force that is much greater than the Elite Systems, which are controlled by a fraction of the 1%.

- Something bigger than system change is unfolding. It is a shift to a higher energy and consciousness.

You can affirm and support change through a shift in your thought patterns. We have talked about letting go of dysfunctional beliefs; we can also strengthen new, positive beliefs. Affirmations can hasten the transition to Home Rule, Common Good Systems as they clarify and reinforce what you want.

Free yourself from dysfunctional beliefs and the distortions of propaganda. Replace them with the understanding that you are empowered to make change. One person can change a nation. Gandhi, and Martin Luther King showed a peaceful path for system change. All you need to do to start is believe.

Belief Reminders

- Under our patterns of behavior, under all that we think, lives all we believe.

- The events of our lives do not determine our realities so much as the decisions that we make about those events. These decisions can form beliefs.

- Our beliefs become unquestioned commands to our nervous systems. They write the script for our perceptions.

- Beliefs shape intention and action. They have the power to expand or destroy the possibilities of our present and future.

- Beliefs can be planted and manipulated, like the Pandemic and the "War on Terror." Also, our memory can be influenced to change its recall. So we may have many false beliefs.

- Whenever we believe something, we no longer question it. Question your beliefs. Question your group's beliefs.

- Breakthroughs in awakenings are triggered with a change in energy-draining beliefs.

- Believe in and think about what you want. Visualize and affirm the change.

BE THE CHANGE IN YOUR COMMUNITY

"Be the change you want to see"—Gandhi

Believe that you can play a role in changing our societal systems, so they serve the common good. Believe in the power of community. By forming community, and working with each other, we can tap into a power much greater than ourselves. By holding love and aspiration in our hearts, we access a naturally high-vibrating power that can be used as a creative force, and the power to change the corrupt system peacefully. We can move into Common Good Systems, where all basic needs, such as medical and education, are paid by tax revenues. We can rewire the deceptive flow of money that is presently going to the elite few, so that more of those revenues serve communities. Through community, we can access real, sustainable wealth.

Non-violent grassroots community organizing is a well-proven and inspiring means of mass social change. It only takes one person who truly believes in their aspiration. These beliefs and goals were fueled by community. Movements in India, the United States, and Poland demonstrate how grassroots initiatives can make monumental shifts, despite social and political environments that oppose that type of organizing.

Mahatma Gandhi, seeing the negative results of more than a century of British rule, set about to reform that system. The strategy of civil disobedience on a mass scale began with homespun cloth and defying the British salt tax, a powerful symbol of engagement, as salt is a necessity for sustaining life. These tax laws placed a great burden on the poor.

Gandhi's protest began with a 240-mile march to the salt beaches, that included dozens of journalists, who provided a world stage. It was well-planned, with speeches scheduled at the villages along his route, for each of the 24 days of the march. It soon gained notice and momentum. By the time of Gandhi's arrest and the bloody protest at the salt works, India had changed as a nation.

Photo of Gandhi at Dandi, gathering salt, April 5, 1930. Millions of citizens realized they did not have to subjugate themselves to a corrupt system and could peacefully refuse to participate. The citizens can co-create a system that serves the communities, instead of an elite few. A powerful force was unleashed that eventually created independence from the British Empire. The symbol of salt now represents India's independence, as tea does for the United States.

Another inspiring grassroots movement began in August 1980. Workers at the Gdansk Shipyard in Poland organized a non-violent strike, led by Lech Walesa. The strike was well-orchestrated and included lines of communication throughout Europe. It quickly expanded to include forty additional factories. Workers demanded free trade unions, the right to strike, and increased wages and benefits, and became unified around their declaration of workers' rights. They formed an organization they named "Solidarity," and worked diligently and strategically, staging rallies and networking. Within four months, Solidarity grew to a group that was ten million strong. This grassroots movement proved to be *too* powerful. Solidarity's constant pressure resulted in the fall of the corrupt communist regime, whose grip had firmly been on the population for sixty long years. Through parliamentary elections, Solidarity defeated the government in power by a vote of 10 to 1.

Our global history is filled with examples of this grassroots power at work. These social shifts happened because people decided to unite around a cause, were well-organized, utilized the public media to their advantage, and had an inspirational leader or team who helped guide strategic action. The real power base is generated by people coming together in community, taking action, and holding the belief that they will achieve their vision.

From the largest movements of social change to the smaller ones involving a town ordinance, power comes from the people. The power of community is a global change agent. Community provides what the ancient tribes knew intuitively. That is where their strength lies.

This power is not a metaphor—it is actually experienced when group endeavors become a conduit for action that will benefit their community. You can find such focused action in a Volunteer Fire Department, where people work in community pantries and meal sites, within a town hit by a natural disaster, or a group searching for a missing child. Once we understand what brings about this heightened sense of working together, we can apply that in our groups' endeavors. By directing that power to the trigger to effect systemic change

The Elite know that by breaking this community connection, they break the only true power that can defeat them. The breaking up of clans, local family farms, neighborhood stores, long-term jobs, and the middle class all contribute to the breaking of community. Now the unprecedented global lock downs and isolation of people while ramping up disinformation. Could this be an effort to disarm community strength? We need to renew our willingness to go back to community-based connections that unite the grassroots.

To become powerful, allow your community to be powered by All!

APPENDIX A

SOCIAL ENGINEERING

A question haunts me, as my awareness of injustice and abuse from the parasitic Elites Corporate Rule increases. How can fractions of 1% of the population get away with perpetrating such atrocities on the 99%? What allows them to keep control? What weaves this curtain of deceit that blocks our view of the truth?

A science, called social engineering, has been exploring these questions of engineering consent for over one hundred years. To grasp what is truly going on, we need to look to the past to understand the present. It is through dealing with the facts that strategies win.

The past illustrates the mechanisms that are being used today. They include resetting nations. The use of propaganda to hide the facts. Creating hypnotic states. The undermining of critical thinking. The use of chemical and biological warfare on the population. Orchestrating debt and fear. Each of these elements are in use right now. Let's go to where we do have facts from the past that illustrate the mechanisms in play now. From this, we can paint a clearer picture of what our society is faced with.

Defining Social Engineering

The primary funding source for this science, the Rockefeller Foundation, explored how to mold society for a certain function, aspiration, and achievement. The science also explores how to dissuade the population from protesting the loss of their rights or accepting the growing class divides.

Humans can then be seen as machines that can be manipulated by the 1% and can create the illusion of a democracy. People can be programmed for certain actions by the push of a button or the sound of a bell; we are malleable and can be redesigned and shaped, even without our awareness.

Virtually all law and governance, which has the effect of seeking to change behavior, could be considered "social engineering" to some extent. Proscriptions on murder, rape, theft, and even littering are all policies aimed at discouraging undesirable behaviors. Governments also influence behavior more subtly, through incentives and disincentives built into economic policy and tax policy, and have done so for centuries.

We are facing something very different than laws that affect behavior. Are we being manipulated to tear up our social fabric and embrace a new social order?

SOCIAL ORDER RESETS

Social engineering is often more apparent in countries with authoritarian governments. In the 1920s, the government of the Soviet Union embarked on a campaign to fundamentally alter the behavior and ideals of Soviet citizens, to replace the old social frameworks of Tsarist Russia with a new Soviet culture in order to create the New Soviet man. The Soviets used newspapers, books, film, mass relocations, and even architectural design tactics to change personal values and private relationships.

Similar examples are: the Chinese "Great Leap Forward," which was an economic and social campaign of the Communist Party of China (CPC) reflected in planning decisions from 1958 to 1961. The aim was to use China's vast population to rapidly transform the country from an agrarian economy into a modern communist society through the process of rapid industrialization and collectivization. Mao Zedong led the campaign based on the Theory of Productive Forces. Chief changes in the lives of rural Chinese included the introduction of a mandatory process of agricultural collectivization. Private farming was prohibited, and those who persisted in engaging in it were labeled

211

as counter-revolutionaries and persecuted. Mao's movement was responsible for 40 million deaths.

Some people think these deaths were a small price to pay. Here is what one of the main architects of social engineering in the United States had to say about China's reset. *"One is impressed immediately by the sense of national harmony.... Whatever the price of the Chinese Revolution, it has obviously succeeded... in fostering high morale and community purpose. General social and economic progress is no less impressive.... The enormous social advances of China have benefited greatly from the singleness of ideology and purpose.... The social experiment in China under Chairman Mao's leadership is one of the most important and successful in history."*-- David Rockefeller, *New York Times*, 8-10-1973.

MEDIA CONSOLIDATION AND CONTROL

Five huge corporations -- Time Warner, Disney, Murdoch's News Corporation, Bertelsmann of Germany, and Viacom (formerly CBS) -- now control most of the media industry in the U.S. General Electric's NBC is a close sixth. They all align with Corporate Rule

The corporate elite in many ways feel like they won over the population when they gained total control of mainstream media. Back in the 90's, that control allowed them to amp up their activities because they have control of the community narrative. They can do what they please and orchestrate what people think. It made the war on terror possible, and now it is the war on everyone.

But there are even more sinister uses of media control. The Elite's most profitable venture, war and the resulting control of national resources, is greatly aided by propaganda. Concerned citizens are asking how a world so sick of bloodshed and a population so tired of conflict could be led to participate in even more wars.

Our global population is now facing a different war, one on society itself. Mainstream media claim this is a war on a virus. Does shutting down businesses, wearing masks, social distancing, and creating hype to get injected with an experimental biological agent make sense? Get the facts and question.

Why were there a big drop in influenza deaths and why were hospitals tagging cancer and trauma deaths as Covd-19? Why are medicines that are simple and relieve symptoms banned? Why are the mega-rich making $billions on the Pandemic? Why is information that doesn't feed the corporate narrative being blocked? Is this a strategy of deception to enforce Corporate Rule and the New World Order? Take a look at the well-greased propaganda machine to see how it works.

THE PROPAGANDA WAR MACHINE

The Elite greatly prosper through war, and the media becomes a platform to justify actions that result in the plunder of countries, all at U.S. taxpayer expense. A centuries-long history[24] of how the media has been used to justify wars is well-documented in the Corbett Report, "False Flags Over Iran", 2012.

The media generates wartime frenzy, dehumanizes the supposed enemies, and manipulates the public into believing in a war for democracy and freedom that later is found to be untrue. Conflicts in Panama, Iraq, Afghanistan and Libya are recent examples and have been extremely profitable to the Corporate Elite, who benefit greatly from the wars they help generate. Here is some insight of public manipulation to justify war.

The US was drawn into World War I by the sinking of the *Lusitania*, a British ocean liner carrying American passengers. The ship was torpedoed by German U-boats off the coast of Ireland, killing over 1,000 passengers. What the public was not informed about at the time was that just one week before the incident, then-First Lord of the Admiralty Winston Churchill had written to the

President of the Board of Trade that it was *"most important to attract neutral shipping to our shores, in the hopes especially of embroiling the United States with Germany."* Nor did reports of the attack announce that the ship was carrying rifle ammunition and other military supplies. Was there an internal explosion involved? Instead, reports emphasized that the attack was an out-of-the-blue strike by a maniacal enemy, and the public was led into the war.

The US involvement in World War II was likewise the result of deliberate disinformation. Although the *Honolulu Advertiser* had even predicted the attack on Pearl Harbor days in advance, the Japanese Naval codes had already been deciphered by that time, and Naval Intelligence knew. Actually, the U.S., which had provoked the attack through naval blockades on Japan, allowed the attack to happen to unsuspecting Hawaiian residents and US military in order to catapult the U.S. into yet another war. History books, however, still portray Pearl Harbor as an example of a surprise attack.

In 1991, the world was introduced to the emotional story of Nayirah, a Kuwaiti girl who testified about the atrocities committed by Iraqi forces in Kuwait, such as removing babies from incubators to die on a concrete floor. This justified the first war with Iraq. What the world was never told was that the incident had in fact been the work of a public relations firm, Hill and Knowlton, and that the girl, actually the daughter of the Kuwaiti ambassador, had aspirations of being an actress. Once again, the public was whipped into a frenzy of hatred for the Hussein regime, on the basis of an imaginary story told to the public via their televisions, orchestrated by a US PR firm.

In the lead-up to the final war on Iraq, the American media infamously took the lead in framing the debate about the Iraqi government's weapons of mass destruction -- not as a question of whether or not they even existed, but as a question of where they had been hidden and what should be done to destroy them. NBC Nightly News asked, "What precise threat do Iraq and its weapons of mass destruction pose to America?", and *Time* debated whether Hussein was "making a good-faith effort to disarm

Iraq's weapons of mass destruction." The U.S. administration later admitted there were no such weapons, but the war was over.

Television stations do not broadcast what they don't want you to hear. They put on what they want you to see. It's an embedded practice that goes back. In 2005, the Bush White House admitted to producing videos that were designed to look like news reports from legitimate independent journalists, and then feeding those reports to media outlets as prepackaged material that was cleared to broadcast on the evening news. When the Government Accountability Office ruled that these fake news reports in fact constituted illegal covert propaganda, the White House simply issued a memo[25] declaring the practice to be legal. So the fake news Trump refers to is not fake.

Similarly, in 2011, shortly after President Obama admitted the presence on the ground in Libya of covert operatives identified as CIA agents by the *New York Times*, he admitted the goal was to destabilize the Gadhafi government. Foreign mercenaries were brought in to kill civilians, and the media then blamed the Libyan government for killing its own citizens. Propaganda was used to justly an invasion by UN allies for "humanitarian reasons." Now, although the entire country is being ransacked, that does not make the news.

Not only does the top-down control of the news make up or distort stories; journalists are being complicit in this manipulation. As the vehicle through which information from the outside world is captured, sorted, edited and transmitted into our homes, the mass media has a huge responsibility.

Media shapes and informs the understanding of events to which we don't have first-hand access. The reporters, producers, and directors have a great responsibility to report the most important news in the most objective way. Aside from a few pockets-of-truth reporters, the major portion of Main Street Media is shaped by the Elite, their agenda, and talking heads.

An informed and engaged public is far less likely to go along with wars waged for power and profit for the Elite few, at taxpayers' expense. And as the public becomes better informed about the very issues that the media has distorted for so long, they realize that the answer to all of the manipulation is to get your news from reliable independent sources, such as the Corbett Report (www.corbettreport.com)

You determine if the present lockdown, social distancing, mask-wearing is effective. Research beyond the illusion of fake news that led us into war. This time it is not a war against nations, or some terrorist, this time it is a war against everyone. We all can be carriers of the enemy virus, and not even know it.

We live in a sociopathic system. How much is orchestrated, and how much is real? Is this virus another form of Anthrax that the US government spread to keep people in fear and submission? Why is there an information war where opposition to the mainstream media is shut down? Who has the right to censor valuable factual information? Is this part of the propaganda war machine now directed at the 99%?

TV HYPNOSIS AND DIVERSION

I asked over 100 activists, during workshops I led, how many of them watch TV. I received a consistent response: 90% did not watch mainstream TV, not wanting to fill their head with made-up stories and propaganda. They didn't want to waste their time numbing out in front of a flickering tube, diverting themselves from the true task at hand. Other news sources, primarily the Internet and radio, are what they rely on. It is interesting that those who renounce mainstream TV have time to get involved in their communities.

TV in Our Life (Pre-Pandemic)

- Number of hours per-day TV is on, in an average U.S. home: 6 hours, 47 minutes[26]
- Number of hours of TV watched annually by Americans: 250 billion
- Number of minutes per week parents spend in meaningful conversation with their children: 3.5
- Number of minutes per week the average child watches television: 1,680
- Percentage of local TV news broadcast time devoted to advertising: 30%; about crime, disaster and war: 53.8%
- Percentage of local TV news broadcast time devoted to public service announcements: 0.7%

Televisions transmit hypnotic flashing lights in a dark room, ideal for generating an Alpha Mind state, similar to a trance. Our brain uses its 8-to-13 cycles-per-second Alpha waves to become idle, to rest areas not actively processing and acting on incoming sensory and motor information. While this idling is a normal and favorable phenomenon, if Alpha wave activity occurs too often, it becomes more difficult to stay focused and be active. TV can cause unfocused daydreaming and the inability to concentrate.

Dr. Erik Peper, another influential brain wave researcher and writer, once said, *"The horror of television is that the information goes in, but we do not react to it. It goes right into our memory pool, and perhaps we react to it later, but we do not know what we are reacting to. When you watch television, you are training yourself not to react and so later on, you're doing things without knowing why you're doing them or where they came from."*[27]

Under the influence of television, the frontal lobe cannot function at its full capacity. The brain does record information: sight, memory, and emotions are all functioning well. Nevertheless, the brain no longer critically analyzes the information. Terrible scenes can be depicted, but the viewer tends only to laugh or shrug them off. Normally, if those kinds of events happened in real life, the individual would be appalled. Even this is changing, however, as people become more desensitized through exposure.

The same hypnotizing brain activity that occurs while watching television also occurs while playing video games. A survey conducted by Akio Mori, a professor at Japan's Nihon University's College of Humanities and Sciences, found that the longer people spent playing video games, the less activity they showed in the prefrontal region of their brain, which governs emotion and creativity. What is even more worrisome is that according to the study, brain activity in the people who continually played games did not recover in the periods when they weren't playing games.[28]

We take in the news and stories that shape our awareness, and absorb them in a hypnotic state that provides emotional pabulum and escape. This influences our society in many ways, and shapes our values and cultural norms. Consider the effect the growing amount of televised sexual content is having on American young people. Documentation shows that the erotic influence of TV and the Internet is so pervasive, it increases sexual activity in teens and younger children. Studies show that the age of first sexual intercourse significantly has decreased due to the influence of TV. The more television watched, the lower the age for that first sexual encounter. Not only do studies show it, children themselves report that television encourages them to take part in sexual activity at a young age.[29]

Since the anthrax attacks in 2001, biological attacks have been increased in mainstream reporting. The anthrax used was manufactured by a U.S. weapons lab. Then there has been the repetitive messaging manufactured through full-length movies and TV. I counted 79 movies all preparing the subconscious for what they want you to believe. Movies like Outbreak, Contagion and The Flu. Is what is happening orchestrated to be a script playing out?

EDUCATION SYSTEM AND THE LOSS OF CRITICAL THINKING

It is too early to assess the full impact of measures taken to shut down schools, the stress on families and the repercussions on the psyche of young impressionable minds. If we are looking to get back to the previous education system, we must be aware of what we are resetting into. Take an objective look at the way it was and can we avoid the shortcomings of this educational system in the reset.

Children are taken from families during their formative years and provided with a certain type of education that reinforces beliefs about supporting Corporate Rule, teaches obedience to authority, and reduces critical thinking. The education system can actually be seen as a factory for creating indifference to intellectual ideas, a factory for obedient workers.

In school, students are given a stream of information that they must memorize in unrelated segments. Like Pavlov's dogs, students then respond to bells and move on to the next class. Different subjects are taught in different classrooms by different teachers, further enhancing segmentation. Segmentation prevents grasping the big picture and is integral to Elite Systems. This does not create an environment to really think about and explore a topic from many perspectives.

The federal government gets to mandate what schools teach, and the testing required by funding just enough of the school operation to make or break the school budget. In western Massachusetts, this is 18% of the school budget. If the school doesn't comply with the "No

Child Left Behind" testing, it will be forced to close its doors, since federal funds would be withdrawn.

Under the present U.S. educational system, there is an absence of critical thinking. Students are taught to simply regurgitate what they are told and are not encouraged to question the information they are fed. However, we really need educated, critical thinkers if we are to sustain a functional democracy.

A functioning democracy requires people to work well with each other, yet that is not taught in school. While conducting hundreds of workshops in teambuilding, I would ask how many had received training, or even had discussions about listening skills, in school. Out of thousands of people asked, I only found eight participants who had some listening training; six of those eight were from private schools. I would scratch my head in wonder. The skill you use the most in life is interpersonal skills. If you want to advance in a job, interpersonal skills are essential. Yet that doesn't even show up on the curriculum?

The goal of education should be to create lifelong learners and critical thinkers, to develop interpersonal skills and collaboration; however, the educational system seems designed to do just the opposite. If you produce students who memorize what they are told, take action only when authority tells them, and compete fiercely among themselves, they will be well-suited for the Elite Corporate Systems, but not for real life. Now more than ever, critical thinking is needed.

CHEMICAL WARFARE

Many strategies are being used to further the trance and the control by the Corporate Elite. For they know that if the masses wake up from their trance, the scam will be over for the 1%. So another method they use involves chemicals that affect our capacity to comprehend, respond, and be active. Four methods of chemical ingestion the elite use are: the water we drink, the air we breathe, the food we eat, and the medicines we take.

Water or Fluoride?

The most widely used chemical in creating subjugation to authority is sodium fluoride.[30] Fluoride not only makes people docile; it also dumbs them down. A Harvard University analysis of 27 epidemiological studies of fluoride in the main water supply concluded that "children in high fluoride areas had significantly lower IQ scores than those who lived in low fluoride areas.[31] The adverse health effects of fluoridated water include brain damage, and infertility. This practice amounts to forced medication of the population, without their knowledge.

Sodium fluoride is used as rat and cockroach poison, and as Sarin Nerve Gas. The American public needs to understand the fact that Sodium Fluoride is a hazardous waste by-product of the nuclear and aluminum industries. Fluoride is also a main ingredient in

225

anesthetic, hypnotic, and psychiatric drugs! So why is fluoride allowed to be added to toothpastes and drinking water?

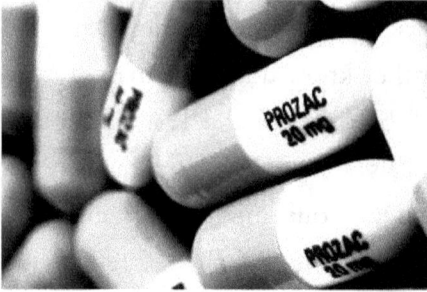

Fluoride is a psychoactive drug that numbs the mind. It is also a basic ingredient in the most popular drug being prescribed: Prozac, scientific name Fluoxetine, which is mostly fluoride. One in six people in the U.S. population is taking some form of Prozac. How does this affect our health? Independent scientific evidence over the past 50-plus years has shown that sodium fluoride shortens our lifespan, promotes various cancers and mental disturbances, and most importantly, makes humans stupid, docile, and subservient.[32]

We are also being attacked by chemicals through the air; most of the United States is being sprayed nearly daily in most regions with long trails of chemicals from high-flying military planes. It is related to HAARP (High Frequency Active Auroral Research Program), a U.S. military weather modification program. The composition of the spray is primarily aluminum oxide, and barium -- among other ingredients. The aluminum does have long-term impacts on health and mental clarity. It is important to find out how much of the extreme weather we are experiencing is derived from black ops weaponizing the weather, versus climate change, derived from CO2 emissions. This is an important consideration if you are concerned with climate change.

Another form of attack is in the foods we eat, especially genetically modified and chemically treated foods. There is a wide range of research on the topic. But the simple solution is to grow your own produce, if possible. The second best is to support local farms that grow healthy and nutritious produce. But the point is, if we utilize the Elite's food chain, we are taking in foods that are low in nutrition. Most importantly, the foods can harm us because of their altered genes, and also the chemical sprays and hormones added. Adding harmful chemicals and modified genes into the food supply lowers people's energy, immune systems, increases obesity, and makes the population more docile.

Glyphosates are in nearly all non-organic foods. They are the herbicides used in Round-Up and now are in the bodies of most U.S. citizens. In enough accumulation, they cause cancer, stillbirths, autism and lower semen count. They are a major health hazard, and their impact is trying to be suppressed by our government, which had strong ties with Monsanto. Now that Bayer has purchased Monsanto, a name change does not eliminate the danger to our food supply. Off-the-shelf wheat products are not only genetically modified, but contain significant glyphosates. *Buy local organic!*

227

THE USE OF FEAR TO MANIPULATE SOCIETY

"When the people fear their government, there is tyranny; when the government fears the people, there is liberty." — *Thomas Jefferson*

In behavioral studies, the driving force scientists used to motivate response was fear. Social engineering is much about influencing a person to take an action due to an emotion that is felt. Instead of talking just about how to manipulate, social engineering causes a target to feel the emotion. Once that emotion is triggered, it can then trigger an action to follow it up.

In the mid-20th century, people in the United States were made to fear the "communist menace." For example, university professors were arrested for discussing Marx's philosophy in their lectures. Hollywood actors who expressed sympathy with socialism or the poor were arrested, and many were jailed. Unions were destroyed because Washington said they were "hotbeds of communism." Homes were ransacked by the FBI and police looking for "communist writings." People were imprisoned for "thought crimes" such as thinking Marx was admirable. The careers and lives of many creative people were destroyed, and the majority of the population, because of U.S. Senator Joe McCarthy and his House Un-American Activities Committee, was kept in a state of perpetual fear.

People who feel exploitation, stress, and disenfranchisement often redirect those feelings toward others. In the South, poor, uneducated white people were told that their problems were due to black people. Their anger and frustrations were then targeted through the KKK (Ku Klux Klan). At other times, abortion, gay marriage, or immigrants crossing the U.S./Mexico border are the targets of hatred. Now it is neighbor against neighbor, as they may be a carrier of this invisible virus.

FEAR

The fear of the virus, social distancing, shut down of businesses, growing disenfranchisements, economic stress, and diminishing options are making many people feel like an emotional volcano that wants to erupt.

"Oderint dum metuant (Let them hate, so long as they fear)" – Caligula, Roman Emperor

When they developed a war on terror, that gave the elite orchestrators the delusional framework to generate a state of continual fear. People's state of anxiety, of pervasive fear, a sense of what is looming, is even worse than the event itself. The war on terror provides a coercive environment that perpetuates fear and anxiety. The Corporate Elite can ratchet up the level of fear through media hype, such as the terror alerts that register yellow, orange, and red used after the anthrax attack. Now they can keep it dialed into the red.

Fear is a useful means to suppress information. National security is the excuse to hide treason. One of the simplest ways to ensure universal fear and mistrust is to announce that "there are enemies amongst us," or now "there is a virus among us" and have people police each other. In such a society, there is universal mistrust -- which is simply a form of fear.

As a counter-measure, it is important that local law officials become educated about the threat to the towns and cities they have sworn to protect. A growing number of law enforcement agents have taken oaths to defend their families, community, and Constitution over federal or state actions that may harm what they have sworn to defend.

The answer is to educate local law officials, who will be called upon to enforce the Elite's decisions, which often go against the Common Good.

Actions to Counter Social Engineering

- Turn off the main-stream TV and reduce video games.

- Become active in your community; civic action is needed.

- Be aware of the water you drink; eliminate sodium fluoride.

- Be aware of foods contaminated by glyphosates. Eat organic.

- Do your best to be happy; reduce fear.

APPENDIX B

FALSE FLAG ATTACKS

The following facts are meant to expose a strategy and a consistent pattern of harm, deception, and reprisals. The parasitic elite are able to extract tremendous wealth and enslave populations to a life of suffering through this strategy. It has been their main mechanism for capturing peaceful countries to pillage the population and resources. It is an inhuman crime that can only be attributed to sociopaths and the systems they create in their own image.

The term "false flag" was derived from the annals of naval warfare, where ships would literally fly the flag of a different nation, pretending to be allies in order to slip past enemy defenses. It is based on deception to obtain a goal. Chapter 1 introduced false flag but it is important to look deeper into its use by a segment of the United States Government.

This global pandemic, its origin, the use of media, the suppression of facts, who benefits and to what ultimate purpose are unfolding. However, we do have a history of how it works within its operating system. This can shed light on the pandemic response, lock downs and repercussions.

This strategy of false flags loses its potency when the truth is exposed. Therefore, this information is meant to nullify one of their main weapons. It is a weapon of great darkness; this darkness cannot exist in the presence of light and truth. The Light needs to burn bright. This awareness, combined with Home Rule, will cause the entire house of cards that the Elite have so cleverly constructed to collapse.

To understand what is unfolding in our global society, take an objective look at this highly successful false flag ploy. Exposure and truth are its enemies, as it encourages appropriate action to prevent a global catastrophe and the manifestation of a global, fascists, sociopathic, suppressive world order.

THE FALSE FLAG FORMULA

Create violence, blame it on others, and use it to gain more power. This is why there are hundreds of documented examples of governments staging attacks in order to blame them on their political enemies.[33] In every civilization, in every culture, in every historical period, authoritarians have known that spectacular acts of violence help to further consolidate their own power and control. It can be used to overtake an entire nation and now being applied to the entire planet.

No one is immune from the disease of avarice and suppression spewing from the elite few who are orchestrating corporate rule.

In Germany, a new Reichstag election was scheduled for early March 1933. Only a few days before the election, on February 27, the Reichstag building was partially destroyed by fire. The Nazis set the blaze, but they blamed the Communists, charging that the Communists were plotting to seize power. Hitler convinced Hindenburg to take strong action against the supposed Communist threat, and the president suspended freedom of speech and the press, and other civil liberties. Later elections swept the Nazis into power. On March 23, 1933, the German Government passed the Enabling Act, which gave dictatorial authority to Hitler's cabinet for four years. Armed with full powers, Hitler moved to eliminate all possible centers of opposition, subordinating all independent institutions to the authority of Hitler and the Nazi Party.

The Russian FSB was caught planting bombs in Moscow in the 1990s during a terror scare that swept Putin into power and stirred the public into supporting the Second Chechen War. [34]Their autocratic President came to power campaigning on the graves of those his old FSB cronies had killed.

The British SAS officers were caught dressing up as Arabs in Iraq, driving around with trucks full of munitions, shooting at police to stir up ethnic tensions and ensure that permanent bases could be built in the region. The captured British agents shown here staged themselves as Sunni's to stir ethnic unrest that would justify the continued occupation by American and British troops.[35]

Haroon Aswat, the supposed mastermind behind the 7/7 London bombings, was working for British Intelligence. British military intelligence took part in the IRA bombings.

The Israeli's Mossad has been caught time and again posing as the very Muslim terrorists they claim to be opposing. Israel uses the specter of terror to further extend their blank check drawn on American funds to expand their police state at home and maintain their hard-line stance against Palestine.

The United States has taken the most brazen and destructive path. Some of the greatest destruction of human life and property this world has ever seen has been perpetrated by the Banksters' covert strong arm. The CIA has sponsored terrorism in the 30 countries using this false flag strategy. The Vietnam war, based on a false flag lie, exemplify the harm they will do to meet selfish goals.

There were smaller incidents associated with legislation. Multiple bombs were found, dismantled and taken out of the Alfred P. Murrah Building on April 19, 1995. [36] This expands the investigation beyond a truck bomber, but was never pursued. Timothy McVeigh had written a letter to his sister in which he claimed to be in the Special Forces for the U.S. Army. They are learning the bombing was being directed by FBI informants, just as the 1993 World Trade Center bombing was. McVeigh's body was never recovered from his supposed execution.

In February 1995, Joe Biden introduced a bill called the Omnibus Counterterrorism Act of 1995. Proposing sweeping changes to American law enforcement, it allowed for secret evidence to be used in prosecutions, expanded wire-tapping by the government, and the creation of "terrorism" as a federal crime that could be invoked to allow the use of the U.S. military in domestic law enforcement, in direct violation to long-standing laws against such measures.

The Clinton Administration was unable to get Biden's bill passed in the wake of the Oklahoma City Bombing tragedy, but it returned in 2001 as the Patriot Act. In the wake of the Patriot Act, all crimes and even misdemeanors could be treated as acts of terrorism, and civil liberties were greatly eroded. Now that Joe Biden is president, what do you think he has in store?

Operation Northwoods and their own Army Counter-insurgency Manuals teach officers how to commit false flag attacks to blame on their enemies. It is a measure crafted by the CIA on foreign soil that came to roost in New York City and Washington, DC.

9/11/2001 TRUTH

This is a powerful example of how society is being manipulated. If you look at the facts the veil of delusion planted in our sub-conscious drops and you can see how nefarious their acts can be. It also puts the present shutdowns, manipulation of data, and vaccines in a clearer perspective.

What happened in New York and Washington, DC, on that day in September? The reasoning and identified perpetrators the government presents do not add up. Their story line is that Osama Bin Laden (a former CIA operative) and his loyal Al Qaeda (name originated by the CIA) army holed up in a cave in Afghanistan brought down the military and financial centers of the United States. Their method was to have a small group of extremists (who had credit cards linked to the CIA) hijack planes armed with box cutters and commit suicide for Allah and the promise of 40 virgins in the afterlife. If you believe their conspiracy theory, then their story and facts do not coincide.

9/11 FACTS; THE WORLD TRADE TOWERS

The three-tower collapses each exhibited the eleven classic characteristics of pre-planned, well-engineered building demolitions, such as collapsing at nearly free fall speed and falling into its foundation. Fire has never, before or after 9/11, caused steel-frame buildings to collapse. This is the only time that a sky- scraper collapsed by a fire, and three occurred on the same day?

The collapse of the 47-story World Trade Center Building 7, a steel- framed high-rise, is highly suspicious, as no plane hit this building and it was the third in history to "collapse from fires alone," the first and second being the WTC Twin Towers. How can a few small fires collapse this building at free-fall speed and have the entire building in a pile at its footprint?

The World Trade Center Towers 1 and 2 center/core areas contained 42 massive vertical support beams. The Commission Report denied their existence to

237

promulgate the now-discredited "Pancake" collapse theory.

The fires in the Twin Towers were not very big, very hot, or very long-lasting compared with fires in several steel-frame buildings that did not collapse.

Office furniture burns at low temperatures of 600- to- 800°F, and that jet fuel, an ordinary hydrocarbon has a maximum burning temperature of 1200°F, but steel melts at 2750°F.

Over one hundred first responders reported many explosions and flashes of light prior to and during the collapse. They heard explosive blasts going off one after the other as the rumbling began, and they ran for their lives. These blasts are integral to controlled demolition.

Mid-air pulverization of 180,000 tons of concrete was not explained. Large volumes of metal decking, floor trusses and "pancaked" floors were also missing.

Blast pressure front effects: multi-ton steel sections ejected laterally – up to 600 ft. away at 50 mph. How can jet fuel poured on steel create this, as the collapse could not account for such projectiles?

The NY fire department and others found several tons of "molten steel flowing like lava" in the ruins. 1400°F office fires cannot produce 2800+°F molten steel/iron. Thermite incendiaries used in control demolitions can.

Microspheres formed from molten iron and other elements were found in the WTC dust by USGS, the RJ Lee Group, EPA, and independent scientists. Thermite reactions account for the ubiquitous spheres.

Information sites that provide lengthy back-up to all statements made in 9/11 facts can be found at: Architects and Engineers for 911truth. www.ae911truth.org, CorbettReport.com. Any books or videos by David Ray Griffin or Richard Gage are recommended.

9/11 FACTS IN WASHINGTON ATTACKS

The Pentagon, the most-guarded airspace on planet, with its own multi-billion- dollar missile defense system was penetrated on 9-11-01.

The 9/11 Commission failed to investigate why the hole in the Pentagon was not even close to resembling the profile of a commercial jet or provide sound scientific evidence of how the large airline engines, along with the passengers and contents, could disintegrate.

Eyewitness testimony said there were no remains of a Boeing 757, either inside or outside the Pentagon. All objective investigators conclude that a plane did not hit, and that it is impossible for such a plane, its titanium engines, and passengers to vaporize, as they claim.

All 85 video tapes in the Pentagon vicinity were confiscated by the FBI, and the few released showed no plane.

The evidence identifies a missile and/or explosives that penetrated the Pentagon.

Tests have shown that cell phone calls with 2001 technology cannot be made at altitudes over 8,000 feet for any meaningful duration and that, more significantly, United Airlines Flight 93 was proven to be 35000-to-40000 feet high when calls were made.

9/11 SET UP

In September of 2000, a group known as The Project for A New American Century (PNAC), many of whom would become key officials in the Bush administration, including Dick Cheney, Donald Rumsfeld, and Paul Wolfowitz, were signatories of a radical military plan, which stated that their goals would not be reached unless a "cataclysmic event, like a new Pearl Harbor" occurred in order to get American citizens on-board with their agenda.[37]

President Bush's brother Marvin and his cousin Wirt Walker III were both principals in the company in charge of security for the World Trade Center.

The 9/11 Commission failed, with over 100 other questions, omissions, inconsistencies and implausible scenarios that fall unacceptably short of the 9/11 Commission's original mandate, constituting gross malfeasance in its overriding obligation to the 9/11 victims' families to conduct a thorough investigation.

Think of Bush standing over the smoking rubble of the Twin Towers declaring a new war on terror, posturing as some hero out to get the bad guy. Still in shock from the horror of the tragedy that has just unfolded before us, a nation can be led into the most ruthless despotism, declaring a new age of global war on terror. Despotism that now bears the shroud of "security."

Nowhere in human history has one event on one day had such reverberations. The pandemic has been spread over months. This one event has justified a perpetual war on terror. Expenditures on that war send trillions of dollars to the military/industrial complex. They have drained the coffers of the U.S. and Iraq. The U.S. had its liberty dramatically taken away by an act of terror on 9/11/2001. Now we are faced with another wave of terror and if you think there was repression in the aftermath of 9/11, imagine what is being contrived on the coat tails of this Pandemic.

LAWS PASSED JUSTIFIED BY 9/11 AND THE QUESTIONABLE COMMISSION REPORT

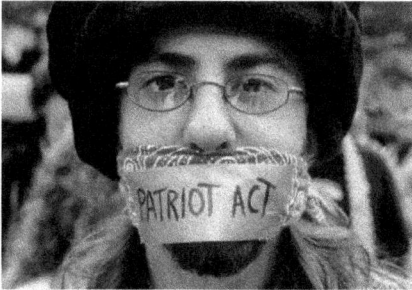

USA Patriot Act. The most anti-Constitution legislation ever passed, pre-authored by Joe Biden. Here are a few things his legislation provides.

- Secretly authorize the NSA to wiretap Americans without probable cause or judicial oversight.

- 2006 Military Commissions Act, which insulated military tribunals from any challenge that they violate the Geneva Convention.

- Revoked habeas corpus rights for "enemy combatants" -- this includes U.S. citizens that this commission deems as terrorists. Torture was "legalized."

- Elevate the President above the law. Resulted in illegal detentions, disappearances, torture.

- July 2007 Executive Order would authorize seizure of property of those accused of supporting the war on terror.

- "Enemy combatants" can be held indefinitely without trial, including dissenters to the U.S. government whom they label as terrorists.

- Suspicious organizations can have their assets frozen without notice or hearings.

- Military tribunals can sentence defendants to death on the basis of hearsay and coerced testimony. They can go after them with drones and missiles.

- The overturning of the venerable Posse Comitatus Act of 1878, which barred the use of active-duty military inside the U.S. for police-type functions.

- The revision of the Insurrection Act to empower the President to take control of state National Guard units, even over the objections of state Governors, and authorize federalization of the National Guard to "suppress public disorder" in the event of broadly-stated occurrences.

- The President has greatly reduced hurdles to the declaring of martial law. That includes medical martial law.

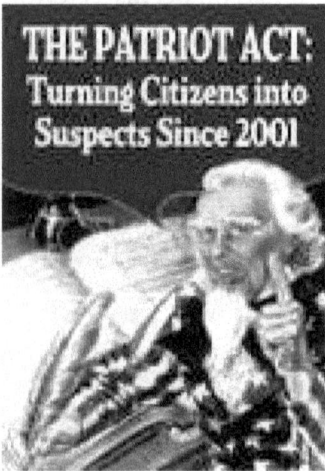

THE PATRIOT ACT: Turning Citizens into Suspects Since 2001

World-wide, the majority of people are more terrorized by the actions of the U.S. administration and its state-sponsored terrorism than by any specific terrorist group.

The (enacted in 2001 and re-approved in 2011) USA Patriot Act is the most sinister of all, in that it violates the first, fourth, fifth, sixth, seventh, eighth, ninth and tenth amendments of the Bill of Rights. In expansion, it grants the government the right to rifle your mail, tap your telephone and inquire into what you are reading. In a stunning overturn of well-accepted fourth amendment rights, a federal court has granted government the right to track your movement with GPS technology, including via cell phones and GPS equipment.

The 9/11 attacks resulted in 2,996 casualties, which included 343 firefighters and 59 police officers who were trying to save victims inside the World Trade Center. A study published in *The Lancet* medical journal estimated that there were 654,965 deaths between 2003 and 2006 – representing 2.5% of the Iraqi population.[38] When you include Afghanistan and Libya it goes into the millions.

There is also the fallout from exposure to depleted uranium. The soldiers, civilians and unborn children have already begun to see the scourge that poisons their being and rivals Agent Orange. Now this pandemic tactic of experimental vaccines has been applied globally, and to what end?

WAR ON EVERYONE

Now the "War on Terror" has become a "War on Everyone." It has morphed into another form of war. Now every person on the planet can carry an invisible pathogen that requires keeping your distance. Whether you believe this was cleverly crafted by man, or that the virus and its cousins were a freak of nature. Whatever you believe, look closely at what is unfolding. The bleak world of George Orwell's book *1984* is upon us if we do not act.

Hopefully, you can see from the past that there has been an ongoing war on society, stepped up since the foothold -- as the Federal Reserve was established in 1913. Now the cancer has infected the upper layers of the hierarchy; it is time to shed the life-sucking diseased parts that have spread to global proportions.

So where is this going? What is the ultimate goal? I will provide a theory based on an experience I had in 2005. At the time, I was a leader in the 9/11 truth movement, pulled in by families of victims who wanted an objective investigation. I was invited with nine other activists to a private home in Connecticut. We were greeted by a large but frail man in his sixties. His oxygen tank was attached to a tube in his nose. He explained that he was dying of radiation poisoning.

He was a former CIA Black Ops agent who got an assignment in Venezuela that resulted in the death of his three compatriots; he was next. The device was supposed to be safe with their protective gear. He was bitter about how they were discarded after the incident. Part of that bitterness and his impending death were motivation enough to disclose the big plan.

"It is a game of subjugation of the population," he explained. *"They have the technology to carry out their plan, but they lacked the necessary deployment."* He informed us about nano technology and that, once in the body, it merges with your organs so it can't be removed. It acts as a transmitter and a receiver. What then activates it is ultra-high frequency. They were planning on developing a high-frequency grid. He said when that gets launched, the next step is not far off. Now we have the 5G grids he referred to in 2005.

"The main problem is getting the nano particles in the body. They tried through aerosol spraying but it would not penetrate the blood stream and cells. The best result is through injection into the bloodstream. There will be a huge push to vaccinate every person on the planet, he said". When I saw the present unfoldment, a cold chill went down my back.

I have no proof that a dying CIA agent in 2005 was not fabricating something, however his sincerity convinced me enough to write about it. The nano technology is presently being used. DARPO Hydrogel has nano particles that fuse with your organs. If this is true, once injected, they can influence recipients of the vaccine through 5G frequency as you are able to transmit and receive signals. I say this to raise caution, not to raise fear. Become well informed before you act.

BE A TRUTH-SEEKER

It is our civic duty to question our governing officials if there is dishonesty, particularly if treason is involved. Realize that to go it alone is futile, and that we need each other. Community is vital on the Common Good Road in front of us. Community is needed to communicate the full scope of the abuse and manipulations that are against our Constitution. Community is needed to gain Home Rule through local elections.

Homeland Security Secretary came out and admitted that the Bush administration had made up terror threats[39] in order to scare the people into supporting the government, so now we know what the real definition of terrorism is. It is governments scaring their own citizens into following the Elite's self-serving agenda. Don't you suspect what is going on is this pandemic fear tactic? Is this about getting people to willingly shut down small and medium size businesses, to increase citizen surveillance, to shut down information on the web, to change all hard currency to digital that others control?

We must realize that the parasitic elite use fear and intimidation. They will create a crisis with a solution that further erodes our freedom and meets their objectives. We must be vigilant, for these tactics are being used now.

Question the impact on weather modification. Question the "official" government data research. Question the death rates due to the pandemic. Question the effectiveness of wearing masks. Question why a new, untried vaccine is being rushed to market.

Being a truth-seeker means accessing literature, videos, and the Internet for the real news. I mentioned several times that a good place to start is podcasts and videos at www.CorbettReport.com. You should question the mainstream media and look for more reliable sources of information.

Truth seekers have become a potential terrorist, according to the governmental and media agencies that deign to limit our range of acceptable opinions and control dissent. However, that stance is powerless as more people become informed. So, increase your circle of influence, and be aware of what is best to engage in.

Marketers and Public Relations experts found that "truth does not rule, perception does." Corporations spend billions to make images, and words evoke certain emotions and shape perceptions. You will need to deal with perceptions fabricated by this elite media, be patient in the education of others.

Truth-seekers can approach communicating truth in a variety of ways. Having a loving and kind disposition makes the truth more acceptable. Each time we provide a different perspective or opposing view, we are confronting the beliefs that our media, educational system, monetary system, and the war machine has spent over one hundred years crafting. Be patient and factual in your discussions.

Being a truth-seeker means you are willing to jettison old beliefs and embrace a deeper truth. It means being willing to engage people where they are at, and be willing to discuss the truth in conjunction with positive action.

Now is the time to act!

REFERENCES

[1] 1984 by English novelist <u>George Orwell</u>. It was published on 8 June 1949 by Secker & Warburg social science fiction novel

[2] Just 8 men own same wealth as half the world. Oxfam Internationa, jan 16, 2017

[3] *IN THE HIGH-ENERGY ZONE: The 6 Characteristics of Highly Effective Groups*, 2002, Paul Deslauriers. Available www.HomeRule.US

[4] *Essays on the Great Depression*. Bernanke, Ben S. (2000). Princeton University Press. p. 7. <u>ISBN</u> 0-691-01698-4. Also *A Monetary History of the United States.*

[5] *The Creature from Jekyll Island: A Second Look at the Federal Reserve*. Griffin, G. Edward (2002). American Media (publisher). ISBN 978-0-912986-39-5.

[6] Clandestine Service History: Overthrow of Premier Ossadeq of Iran, Mar. 1954: p iii.

[7] *Mohammad Mosaddeq and the 1953 Coup in Iran* Edited by Mark J. Gasiorowski and Malcolm Byrne June 22, 2004

[8] *The Looting of America* by Les Leopold

[9] Productivity and the Workweek by Erik Rauch

[10] *55 Reasons Why The U.S. Economy Is NOT On The Right Track In 2012* By: ETF Daily News   Friday, February 24, 2012

[11] *The Level and Distribution of Global Household Wealth,* April 2008, James B. Davies,1 Susanna Sandström,2 Anthony Shorrocks,2 and Edward N. Wolff3 Economics Dept, University of Western Ontario; 2 UNU-WIDER, Helsinki;

[12] The Politics of Obedience: The Discourse of Voluntary Servitude Paperback – May 14, 2015 by Etienne de la Boetie (Author)

[13] War on Terror clips, James Corbett, www.CorbettReport.com

[14] The Lives of Twelve Caesars, the Life of Nero, 38 (c. 121); Tacitus, Annals, XV (c. 117) Cassius Dio, Roman History, Books 62 (c. 229); Suetonius,

[15] False Flags Don't Fly Anymore , James Corbett, The Corbett Report , Apr 19, 2010

[16] Media Manipulation and the Drums of War: How Media is used to Whip the Nation into Wartime Frenzy By James Corbett Global Research, January 03, 2012

[17] *Strip and Flip Disasters of America's Stolen Elections,* by Robert Fitrakis and Harvey Wasserman. Paperback – January 1, 2017

[18] *In the High Energy Zone: 6 Characteristics of Highly effective Groups* January 2001, Paul Deslauriers, NRG Publishing available HomeRule.US

[19] Robert C. Schmitt, "New Estimates of the Pre-censal Population of Hawaii," Journal of the Polynesian Society 80.2 (1971):237-43; Robert C. Schmitt, The Missionary Censuses of Hawaii, Pacific Anthropological Records, 20 (Honolulu: Department of Anthropology, B. P. Bishop Museum, 1973); Kirch, Feathered Gods and Fishhooks 286f

[20] *"Re: Imaging Change"* by P. Reinsborough and J. Smucker; 2017

[21] Maui News Nov. 8, 2018 After election shakeup, dust begins to settle for new council

22 Foundations of Physics June 1973, Volume 3, Issue 2, pp 139–168 Quantum theory as an indication of a new order in physics. B. Implicate and explicate order in physical law David Bohm

23 *The Computer and the Universe*, J. A. Wheelers, The International Journal of Theoretical Physics, (1982)

24 An excellent resource www,CorbettReport.com Excerpts used, refer to JAN. 2012
Faking It: How the Media Manipulates the World into War

25 issued *Washington Post* Mar 15, 2005 [incomplete information – page, section?]

26 *How to Add Twelve Years to Your Life*, The Donella Meadows Archive [publisher, year?]

27 *Four Arguments for the Elimination of Television,* E. Peper, as cited in J. Mander, (New York, NY: Quill, 1977): 211.

28 *Study Suggests: More Game Less Brain*, www.megagames.com (September 7, 2002). http://www.megagames.com/news/study-suggests-more-game-less-brain

29 E. Hundt, Chairman of the Federal Communications Commission, delivered before the National Press Club, (Washington, DC: July 27, 1995).

30 *The Crime and Punishment of I.G. Farben* by Joseph Borkin

31 *Impact of Fluoride on Neurological Development in Children* A Choi and P Grandjean, Harvard University, *Environmental Health Perspectives* July 20, 2012

32 *The Truth About 'Fluoride' (or what every Mother should know)* By Dr. A. True Ott The Journal of History, August 2000

33 *FALSE FLAGS DON'T FLY ANYMORE* , JAMES CORBETT, THE CORBETT REPORT , APR 19, 2010

34 *FBI TERRORISTS, 9/11 UPDATES, BAD WEEK TO BE A BANKSTER - SUNDAY UPDATE, JAMES CORBETT, MARCH 2010 , CORBETT REPORT*

35 *British Special Forces Caught Carrying Out Staged Terror In Iraq? Media blackout shadows why black op soldiers were arrested* Paul Joseph Watson | September 20 2005

36 *Bomb Damage Analysis of Alfred P. Murrah Federal Building.* by Brigadier Gen. Bentin K. Partin, USAF (Ret.), Physics 911

37 The Project for the New American Century. By William Rivers Pitt, 2/25/03

38 *The Human Cost of the War in Iraq: A Mortality Study, 2002–2006* By Gilbert Burnham, Shannon Doocy, Elizabeth Dzeng, Riyadh Lafta, and Les Roberts. A supplement to the October 2006 Lancet study.

39 Made up terror threats Huffington Post August 20, 2009

ONGOING SUPPORT AVAILABLE

WWW.HOMERULE.US

BE PART OF THE EVOLUTION UNDERWAY

ONGOING SUPPORT AVAILABLE

WWW.HOMERULE.US

BE PART OF THE EVOLUTION UNDERWAY

www.ingramcontent.com/pod-product-compliance
Lightning Source LLC
Chambersburg PA
CBHW062207270326
41930CB00009B/1676